The history and techniques of

PUNTING

in Cambridge

R·T·RIVINGTON

OLEANDER PRESS

The Oleander Press
16 Orchard Street
Cambridge
CB1 1JT

www.oleanderpress.com

A CIP catalogue record for the book is
available from the British Library.

ISBN: 9780906672389

Designed and typeset by Hamish Symington
www.hamishsymington.com

Printed in England

Punting in Cambridge   *1*

Techniques of Punting   *26*

The History of Punts   *74*

Punting in Cambridge

THAMES PLEASURE PUNTS did not arrive in Cambridge till about 1902–4. The precise date is not known, though it is within living memory. Don Strange, born in 1895, of the third generation of a family of Cambridge boat builders, remembered the first two Thames punts, both privately owned, brought from the Thames by their owners, one kept at Dolby's and the other at Strange's yards. He could give the year no more precisely than by saying it was after he had started going to school. In *Victorian and Edwardian Cambridge* the caption of an illustration of Bullen's boat-yard says that punts were first brought to Cambridge by Thomas Prime who had seen them raced at Henley. Prime was Dolby's manager at the Anchor yard. The first record of punt racing at Henley was in the Town Regatta in 1901. The information came from Prime's son, who was a neighbour of F.A. Reeve, the book's author. The caption gives the date of the illustration and the punts as about 1880 but this is mistaken for Bullen's yard was not in existence till after 1904. Enid Porter in *Cambridgeshire — Customs and Folklore* says, "Punts did not appear on the river until early this century; by 1907 they had largely replaced the rowing boats for river outings and picnics." Pleasure punts therefore, did not reach Cambridge till comparatively late, but when they arrived their popularity increased so rapidly that they very shortly became the leading pleasure craft.

The family of B.F.H. Dammers believes that he and a friend, S.E. Howard, were the first to build and own a pleasure punt in Cambridge. Dammers and Howard, undergraduates at Pembroke College, came up in 1895. Unenthusiastic about college sport, they sought their own recreation and had their punt built for this purpose. It was a saloon punt, cheaply built, with upright knees; its shortness anticipated the subsequent design of Cambridge punts. The family has a photograph of it, probably of about 1920; Dammers, who had presumably returned to Cambridge with Howard and found the punt again, is standing forward of the deck in the customary position for Thames punters, not that usually adopted at Cambridge. This could support the belief that if they had punted previously at Cambridge, it was before punting was a common practice there. Howard was said to have spent family holidays on the Thames punting before going up to Cambridge. Dammers, father of the present Dean of Bristol, was grandson of a Hanoverian adjutant general who married into a rope-making family of Bridport, a town once with a monopoly of the trade: Dammers was familiar with boats and able to draw designs. The crude design of the punt suggests less experienced work. Dammers who retired to Cambridge was said to have last seen the punt about 1948. He had once had a sailing punt on the Norfolk Broads.

Cambridge is on the south edge of the Fens, a large system of water-ways and levels forming the main part of the basin of the Great Ouse and covering much of the western part of East Anglia. To the north east, in Norfolk, is another large, separate system of waterways and levels, the Broads. Before transport of goods devolved on the railways, Cambridge relied on Fen waterways for heavy goods reaching it. Since the town was at a remote end of the system, it was important the last stage should be kept open to transport. The Cam Conservancy was established by statute, therefore, in 1702, to keep the river Cam navigable over the last few miles from Clayhithe Ferry (but now from Bottisham Lock) to the mills and warehouses around Mill Lane, the old commercial centre of the town. In the town and on the river bank at the back of the colleges there were also a number of hithes or loading places for goods. The Cam Conservators were entrusted with the navigation rights as well as the conservancy duty; barges had to pass through college grounds along the Backs to reach the mills; since there was no tow path, a causeway or paving was maintained along the bed of the river, to form a suitable bottom for horses, breast-deep, hauling the barges up the river. The Backs are still paved in places, leaving little grip for the shoe of a punt pole. These places are few, but the Backs remain shallow, with a firm bottom, excellent for punting. When it was not possible to tow barges up, they were pulled up by watermen with oars called "spreads".

At the mills there was a sluice with a change of water levels. A concrete water-slide was provided, probably about 1911, for hauling boats from one level to the other. The two mills on the right (or Cambridge) bank, King's Mill and Bishop's Mill, were pulled down in 1928. A weir was built, a scheme for beautifying the area was carried out, Granta Place replaced the water-edge where the mills had been and rollers were installed at the slide for moving craft more easily from one river level to the other. The angle of incidence of the rollers is very steep, a rise of two feet in ten, or 1:5; the angle of the slide was probably not altered when the rollers were added to it. There is furthermore a 13ft gap between the two rollers striding the towpath; consequently punts are liable to damage when carried over the rollers and punt-owning watermen restrict hirers in transporting punts over them.

The river above the weir, the upper level, is called the Granta. It is convenient to distinguish the two levels of the river by different names. The navigation rights of the Granta belong to the riparian owners, mainly colleges, for much of the river passes through college land. Below the weir is the Cam and the weir is a limit of the *vires* of the Conservators for its navigation; through their authority, with a special bye-law for that section, requiring them to conserve it as an amenity, not as a navigation, extends from the weir up to Byron's Pool. Granta may have been the old name for the whole of the River Cam. The town was formerly called Grantebryce, corrupted to Cambridge, and "Cam" taken from the new name of the town. As often to be expected, the river above the weir is deeper than the river below it. The depth of water in the Backs is controlled by Jesus Lock, the lock at Jesus Green, below Magdalene Bridge and beyond the north end of the university.

Below Jesus Lock the reaches of the river are rowed on by college eights. The presence of punts is inconvenient for eight-oared boats and it is unusual for punts to go down there, though at one time they were plentiful on it. H.C. Banham had punts for hire there till 1952. However, power boats had become common by the 1930's; because of this Banham began to build punts with high freeboards (the height of craft above the water line), to help resist the wash of motor-boats.

There is a right for any craft to navigate the Backs, since the navigation rights are in the possession of the Cam Conservators whose duty it is to keep the navigation open. The Conservators, who include representatives of the university, consider the interests of the owners

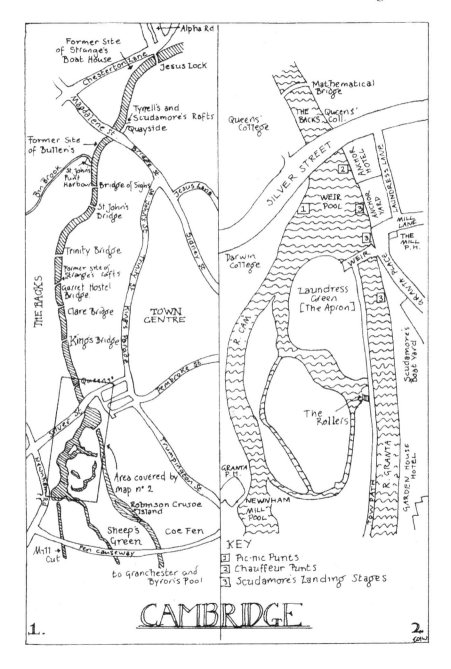

KEY

1 Pic-nic Punts
2 Chauffeur Punts
3 Scudamore's Landing Stages

CAMBRIDGE

1.

2.

of the river, the colleges; so it is therefore difficult to take powered boats above Magdalene Bridge, or even above Jesus Lock except by showing very good reason for it and by justifying the nuisance to the satisfaction of the Conservators.

The extent of the river at Cambridge is far less than at Oxford. The Cam is carefully controlled and managed and there is enough for the needs of Cambridge; nevertheless, space can at times be confined, and this particularly so on the Backs at popular times in fine weather. It is probable that fewer undergraduates learn to punt at Cambridge than at Oxford and punting may be more often regarded at Cambridge as an opportunity for fun and a frolic rather than for rest and leisure. The dean of St John's College has special rules to restrain the action of members of his college with windows above the Backs who are annoyed by the noise of punters. During the 1920's and 1930's, it was understood that a fairly high standard of presentableness and decorum was observed on the Backs. It was expected that those who used it should punt well and dress well, usually in white. This standard was not expected on the Granta or below St John's College. Perhaps the standard was set by how behaviour would be expected in a garden, for the Backs are parts of the college gardens, and a garden may or not be for play, as custom dictates. Since that period, the Backs have been used much more as a playground. A study of the environment of the Cam, *River Cam*, published by the City Architect's Department (1973) said: "On a good summer's afternoon the amount of activity is enormous and occasionally very noisy, but is very much part of the Cambridge scene." The proximity of the river to the colleges and to bystanders in the gardens, cannot but induce a feeling of fun and games into punting on the Backs; in comparison, punters at Oxford are remote. In the comparatively confined space, it is tempting and easy to snatch the pole from a punter passing under a low bridge, or from a punter travelling in the opposite direction as punts are passing close together, or even to push another punter in the river. This kind of behaviour is usually accepted with good feeling. Snatching a pole as two punts pass can be very amusing if done so that the punter losing it is caught so unaware that he is left still perplexed by what has happened even after he has lost it. Snatching poles from several punts may invite trouble, and a public, crowded river will invite misbehaviour. Before the introduction of punts on the Cam, there had been a tradition of rudder-snatching, particularly on the crowded river at the May races, and there had in the end to be a limit to the amount of tolerance it could receive.

Women at Girton and Newham in the 1920's and 1930's were provided with punting lessons by fellow-members of the college but these were not compulsory as at Oxford, for punters. A pick up in three was taught, for this can be as well done standing on the deck as in the punt.

At one time marsh or fen punts were found at Cambridge. These were double-stemmed, about 16ft long and 4ft wide, with a slightly curved bottom, clinker-built, and a low freeboard. The double-ended, working fen and broadlands punts and Dutch *punter* were similar in appearance and use, but differed in the local methods of building. They were of shallow draft; double-ended, they did not have to turn round in narrow channels; with a low freeboard, they kept out of the winds. Similar in function, they evolved separately. They were usually propelled with a quant. A quant differed from a punt pole in that it had a cross-piece at the end shaped to fit under the armpit when shoving with it. A historian of the Broads has said: "Unlike a Thames punt pole, it (the quant) is not trailed along after a stroke, but lifted out of the water and swung forwards. Most of the steering is done before and during the stroke and less after it." His statement is not true of the Thames punt pole which is also used to steer the punt during the stroke. Steering by trailing the pole behind is more often the practice in Holland, Tübingen and Cambridge. The term "shove" is used on the Broads as well as on the Thames. Other Broadland craft shoved with a quant were the Norfolk keel, the Norfolk wherry and the reed lighter. (The Norfolk wherry was a sailing barge, whereas the Thames wherry was a fast rowing boat.) The fenman's punt was sometimes built with a high freeboard and a wet well for use as a fishing punt. There is an illustration of one of these punts (though not double-ended) by a celebrated cartoonist, Henry Bunbury, called "Fishing in 1811". A copy of it hangs in the Anchor Hotel, Cambridge. The town in its background is not Cambridge, for it has a domed building, and Cambridge is without one. Bunbury however was an East Anglian and drew many cartoons of Cambridge. His companion cartoon of a Thames fishing punt, also of 1811, hangs in the Perch Inn at Binsey, near Oxford. There are now no more fen punts in the Cambridge area; the last builder of them was Dunnett of Burwell.

A work-punt still used on the Cam is of a design that probably dates from before the turn of the century. There are about thirty of these punts at Ely in the ownership of the East Anglian Water Board. They are 16ft long, with shallow swims and cross-planked on the bottom. Huffs at each end and a thwart across the centre give strength to the box part of the frame; but the main strength of the punt is given by fore-and-aft planks or broad strakes over the top of the cross-planking, so that the double thickness of the bottom provides a very solid platform on which the rest of the punt is built.

Small work-punts, often called "garden punts", seem to have been familiar river craft in Cambridge before Thames punts arrived. There is an illustration of three Cambridge undergraduates in a punt of this design in The Copper Plate Magazine of 1792. This design of punt lasted in Cambridge until recently and is described by one of the Darwin family of Newnham Grange, Gwen Raverat, formerly Miss Darwin, in *Period Piece* (Newnham Grange is now part of Darwin College). Gwen Raverat says the family, "grew up knowing how to manage boats by instinct: row-boats and canoes; but not punts, for there were then none on the Cam. We had the best of games in an old, square flat bottomed boat, which the gardener used when he was cutting weeds on the river; it always needed bailing and sometimes sank under our very feet." Gwen Raverat's younger sister, Margaret Keynes in *A House by the River* describes the same craft, "there was always, and still is, a garden punt generally kept moored near the landing stage. In the summer months it was frequently needed to rescue balls hit into the river from the lawn above.... The punt was also used as a kind of water-borne cart or floating wheelbarrow in the shallow waters between the house and the islands, or as a vessel from which river weeds could be cut by scythe. It was frequently water-logged and needed constant bailing-out. The two flat ends might be used as seats, but except for having a flat bottom it bore little resemblance to the elegant slim punt of today. It was not until after the turn of the century that Cambridge began to have pleasure-punts. It was believed, erroneously, that the bed of the river was too muddy to allow of punting: no doubt this was a theory originating in Oxford, the home of punts. It was only in Edwardian times that the punt was established as an institution at Cambridge and began to take the place of the Rob Roys, the Canadian canoes, and even the rowing boats."

The son of the last of the fen-punt builders, Dunnett of Burwell, was apprenticed to Banham about 1916. He built some garden punts

Charles Darwin's grandchildren amusing themselves in a garden punt at Newnham Grange (now Darwin College) about 1895.

to order for estates in different parts of the country and when they became better known, they were advertised and sold through the Country Gentlemen's Association. A punt of this design is now made of glass fibre and sold by Salter of Oxford. Unlike the Thames punt built on a frame like a ladder, the frame of this kind of punt is like a box. Banham, however, were less interested in punts. They were builders of racing boats, motor launches and even scientific equipment.

Don Strange believes that the first Thames punt built in Cambridge was built at his father's yard by a Sam Strange, a cousin. The design was copied from a Thames punt with raked knees and Strange thereafter always built punts with raked knees. John Strange, his father, had a fine two-storey wooden boat house between the river and Chesterton Road, opposite Alpha Road. The family had been boat-building since 1865. He also had yards and other properties in Alpha Road. Because the boat yard had no shoring-beam, the bottom of the punt was built last, unlike the traditional method of building punts on the Thames, where the bottoms were laid down first and shaped under a shoring-beam. Strange shaped the sides first, joined them at the correct spacing with temporary struts, made the knees and treads, turned the punt over and clamped (or cramped) the bottom boards into shape, finally making the huffs and deck. The bottom boards today are also clamped at the Cherwell Boat House, since it uses no shoring-beam; but the punt is not turned over. By 1914, Strange had about fifty pleasure punts and four narrow punts, probably T.P.C. regulation size. Don Strange, as a young man, was taught to punt by J.A.C. Croft, who was an undergraduate of Trinity College from 1907–1911. Croft came from Maidenhead and won the Thames Amateur Punting Championship in 1913. To teach Strange, Croft removed the saloon and taught him from the centre of the punt, as for racing. Many undergraduates hired punts by the term. Strange is sure that the practice of punting standing on the deck was introduced by Girton undergraduates and recalled their striking appearance when they first adopted the elevated position. John Strange also had rafts for hiring punts at Trinity College, below Garrett Hostel Bridge. Strange paid no rent to the college before 1914, but there was a strict understanding that rafts and punts were all taken away on Sundays. Eventually a small rent was paid, but the college no doubt regarded having the punts there as the provision of a service.

Dolby was the other well established firm that went into punt-hiring from the time of the time of the introduction of punts. Their manager was Thomas Prime who looked after the boat-hiring, though Prime himself was not a boat builder. Adjacent to the Anchor was a granary,

Strange's Boat House on the Chesterton Lane bank of the Cam, opposite Alpha Road. It fell into disrepair after 1940, when Strange's business was sold.

built about 1840. Pye, the wireless manufacturers took the lease of this from 1899–1913. Dolby took over the building when Pye moved out and from 1914 to 1920 it was known as Dolby's Boat Building Works. By 1922 it had been taken over by Scudamore (who had earlier occupied premises in Mill Lane on the other side of Laundress Lane), who was presumably on good terms, since he quotes the Anchor's telephone number in the directory. Dolby had held the Anchor Boat Houses and the Anchor itself since 1897. From 1912 Mrs. Dolby also had boat sheds on the east side of Laundress (alias Saunders or Anchor) Lane and she continued to hold these after Scudamore had taken over the Boat Building Works. F.H. Dolby's predecessor at the Anchor, Thomas Robson, was like him described as a boat proprietor and the premises described as the Anchor Boat Houses, his wife Sarah being the licensee of the public house. Presumably then it was Robson, who was there from 1890, who developed the boating side of the establishment; though in 1874, a boatbuilder, Mark Johnson, is listed at the same address. Before that (1855–67), the Anchor was simply a beer-shop. In 1816, it was known as the Anchor, a name often used on commercial waterways, and previously as the Dye House, suggesting a connexion with the local work of laundering.

Above the weir Dolby had punts for hire at Sheep's Green or Robinson Crusoe Island, above the site of the present Garden House Hotel. Strange had competed for the lease of this site. When Dolby died about 1906, Mrs Dolby remarried but continued for a long time to run the business herself and in the name of Mrs Dolby.

F. Scudamore went into punt building and hiring assertively in 1906. He advertised his business well and described his punts as Thames punts; his hiring stations were at Mill Lane and Magdalene Street. Others who were building or hiring punts before 1914 were F.W. Bullen in Fisher's Lane, now part of Magdalene College; H.C. Banham at Abbey Road on the lower Cam and later at Jesus Lock; E.H. Mathie, who had worked for Strange and to whom Don Strange had been apprenticed; his punts were hired at Bridge Street but he moved his yard in 1931, when Magdalene College was extended, to Water Lane, Chesterton, a yard now occupied by Two Tees (M. Tyrrell and E. Tyler), former Banham employees, who are still building punts there. Finally there was George Reynolds who began hiring punts from his pavilion and pleasure gardens, the Belle Vue Gardens, on the site of the Garden House Hotel. The gardens, with tennis courts and miniature golf, also provided punts with tea hampers and even gramophones for hire. The Garden House had been a miller's house. It was bought by Reynolds in 1923 for use as a boarding house, became the Belle Vue Hotel in 1926 and was extended in 1936. George Reynolds died in 1957. The hotel was damaged by fire in 1972 and with an ambitious rebuilding programme caught by a time of general financial retrenchment it went into liquidation. As a company, with the business also of F. Scudamore, now Scudamore Boatyards Ltd., it is now in foreign ownership, as the Garden House Hotel.

The early part of the inter-war years were satisfactory for punt hirers and it was a time when punting is remembered with great pleasure by former Cambridge men. The practice of standing on the deck to punt seems to have been well established. The punt was at least being punted bow first. The practice of standing on the till at Oxford had been tried before 1880 and abandoned in favour of punting stern first. The Cambridge men who punted from forward of the deck may have been those who had learnt on the Thames, as some of them have said. Banham noticed that when there was a choice between longer and shorter punts for hire, the shorter were usually selected; he therefore began building punts shorter; he also began to build punts cross-planked on the bottom, though as with garden punts and other work-punts in the locality, this may have been the traditional method of building them.

On the death of F. Scudamore in 1939, George Reynolds bought the business and continued to use his name. The stock list at the purchase included 71 punts, 45 canoes, 140 poles and 338 paddles; Scudamore also stored 35 privately owned punts. The previous four years had been hard ones for boat-hirers, partly caused by bad weather in summer seasons. In 1940, Dolby and Strange sold their businesses to George Reynolds; Strange received £600 for his. When Bullen and Banham ceased hiring punts in the early 1950's, Reynolds had the monopoly of punts for hire in Cambridge, operating all the punts under the name of Scudamore. Reynolds employed S.J. Tyrrell who saw the opportunity for competition and began his business as a punt builder and punt hirer in 1956. Scudamore and Tyrrell remain the only two commercial punt-hirers in Cambridge, Tyrrell at Quayside, by Magdalene Bridge, where Scudamore also has rafts.

The date of the origin of the Damper Club is unknown. Its earliest extant record is its challenge to a punt relay race posted in Oxford in 1952. It may have existed earlier, possibly very much earlier, sinking and resurfacing from time to time, like many informal and unofficial college and university clubs. The president for 1961–2, Dr Graham Chapman said when asked: "I have a vague feeling that the club dates back quite a long way but that could be anywhere from 1882 to 1924." The club was never registered with the proctors until 1971.

In purpose and constitution it was somewhat similar to the Charon Club at Oxford, a very informal social club interested in the river and punting, with the membership requirement of having fallen into the river from a punt fully clothed. Its name appears to have changed from Damper to Dampers about 1958. The Varsity Handbook for 1972/3 describes it: "Dampers Club: The Dampers exists as a social club for all those who have unwillingly entered the Cam fully clothed. During the Michaelmas and Lent terms the Club holds a variety of social functions (alcoholic), with any form of water borne activity, including regular punt jousting, during the summer. The club meets at 'The Anchor' every Sunday evening. The subscription is £1 for life." Like the Charon Club in Oxford, it also regards itself as responsible for the interests of punting in Cambridge.

From 1953, the Dampers Club arranged teams for punt relay-races against the Charon Club, until punt-hirers refused to allow the use of punts for them. Some of the bridges on the Backs are low enough for men standing on them to catch the tops of punt poles when near to a bridge, a perennial Cambridge amusement. When the races were held on the Backs, pole picking from the bridges was a hazard from which Oxford of course suffered worse than Cambridge. For the Oxford team, the experience would probably be unexpected; for all the bridges in Oxford are too high for this.

The minute book of the Damper Club from 1960 is extant. A note on its title pages says: "now alias Dampers". Another note reports the loss of the previous minute book, believing it to have left "for the same damp resting place its successor is likely to find". The club eventually adopted a motto: *per arduum ad alveum*, "through difficulty to the river bed." Annual General Meetings were once held at the Garden House Hotel, then for a long time at Grantchester; a convoy of punts would travel up for lunch there. At least once it was held on the Backs, and finally at the Anchor Hotel.

The Damper Club always maintained an active winter programme. The closest association was with the Archimedeans (the Cambridge University Mathematical Society). Every year there were tiddleywink matches, probably the Archimedeans' choice of game, and once a tiddleywink race across the Bridge of Sighs. They had fixtures against the Austin Seven Club, the Referees Society, the Cambridge City Librarians and women's college teams, for games of bar billiards, monopoly, hockey and netball. Their regular winter sport was pooh sticks, once, for example: "a Knockout Pooh Sticks Championship. The course will be from John's Old Bridge to the Bridge of Sighs. The winner will receive a bottle of port and sticks are to be chosen by the entrants." Apart from the Charon Club match, the summer sport was punt-jousting which took place every Sunday afternoon, and in this the Archimedeans would often join them. Later there were underwater bicycle races and underwater pram races (two or three prams were lashed together and paddled through shallow water). The Dampers Club suggested that all its members should support the Madrigal Concert on the Backs for which the performers were carried in and sang from punts.

In March 1960, in aid of World Refugee Year, the Damper Club challenged London University and the Charon Club to an overland punt race from London to Cambridge, the punts to be mounted on pram carriages and to carry a woman passenger. A member of the Cambridge team, Graham Chapman, Damper chairman in 1961–2 and later of the Monty Python group, recalled it: "Oxford, Cambridge and London Universities competed pushing their punts on pram wheels. This took the worst part of two days, with six hours compulsory sleep… on which London University cheated, as they did also by not following the exact route, to become dubious victors. The real victors were both Oxford and Cambridge who with no connivance (well a bit really) produced an exhausting neck and neck finish. Only six pushers or pullers per team allowed … guess who cheated on this as well? For most of the journey Cambridge were down to three men including my idiotic self (the others were looking for new pram wheels). I have never *ever* and ever EVER indulged in such an exhausting activity in all my life… bent over at the back of a punt staring at the road mile after v. long mile pushing a punt with compulsory female passenger on a 70 mile rant. It would have made Germaine Greer seem like a doddle." Tim Lusty, a member of the Charon team and later Charon president said he began to take an interest in refugees as a consequence of this race and made a career in Oxfam; he also married one of his batons.

In 1968, the Dampers began to look for opponents (apart from the Charon Club) outside Cambridge. They had played netball matches against Homerton and Girton teams, so arranged a pooh-sticks match

17

in January 1969 with a Bishop's Stortford women's teachers' college team formed for the purpose, the Hockerill Suspenders Club (motto: *ad fastigia venimus* "We come to the slopes.") The Dampers offered immediate membership to any Suspender who willingly fell in; the Suspenders stipulated that any who fell in must be accompanied by a Damper who would afterwards provide dry clothing. There was a return match in netball. The Dampers also wrote to the Central Council for Physical Recreation, with copy-letters to the Thames Conservancy and the Sports Council enquiring about, "Boating Clubs on the River Thames who possess punts and take an active interest in punting", since they had heard of but had not been able to find information about them in reference books.

The Thames Conservancy replied, giving addresses of both the Wraysbury and the Dittons Skiff and Punting Clubs. The Dampers sent challenges to both, for relay races on the Cam in King's and Trinity punts, with teams of eight, human batons and a course of about 100 yards. The Wraysbury Club, puzzled or cautious asked for more particulars. The Dittons Club accepted and suggested races for both men's and women's teams also, if possible. All the Dampers' correspondence finished with the club's customary conclusion, "Yours in submergence", and might at first sight have looked a hoax. The Dittons team were invited to dinner in different colleges, but when they eventually formed a party of participants and spectators of sixty, this plan was abandoned. The Dittons Club easily won the first race, and for the rest of the afternoon, teams and spectators divided up in different ways for further races and other events. (Canoe-punting or dongola races might have been appropriate.)

After 1973, the end of Damper v. Charon Club races, the activities of the club declined. In 1977, the committee noted that all club members

Cartoon of the Backs about 1914. Three punters are standing on the deck, a position said to have been introduced by women from Girton. The fourth is standing forward of the deck, the accepted position for the Thames. Gramophones, probably more associated with Cambridge than elsewhere, could be hired from Reynolds. The punt with gramophone is probably not under way.

were third-year men only; they blamed in part a widely published list of university bodies, including the O.T.C. and the Investors Society, considered "wet". Though by the end of the year they had found three new members, there were no minutes for 1978. In the Michaelmas Term 1982, there was renewed interest in the existence of the club and in January 1982, to an enquiry about the club, the junior proctor replied that registration had ceased after 1977 and he advised re-registration if it were re-established. This was done and the new club was active by the Trinity term; jousting and punt racing were again arranged with the Archimedeans who had preserved the old minute book and from whom membership of the new club was drawn. The club also found an undergraduate group at Trinity College, Oxford, interested in punting and challenged them to an amphibious punt race between Cambridge and Oxford, by river and road, using pram wheels on the roads, as in the World Refugee Year race. This was soon seen as impractical; but at the start of the vacation, the two groups met in Oxford and made a joint two-day journey up the Thames.

Whereas in Oxford almost every college makes a block booking for the summer term of punts used without further payment by its Junior Common Room members, punts are not always so easily available in Cambridge to undergraduates. All six undergraduate colleges on the Backs have their own punts and undergraduates in these colleges who punt are fortunate. The number of their punts in use may vary according to which are usable, but are approximately Magdalene – 2; St John's – 12; Trinity – 15; King's – 7; Queens' – 4; Clare – 2. Undergraduates from other colleges have to hire them at the going rate. This may make punting at Cambridge less of a normal college activity than at Oxford.

St John's College has built a magnificent punt harbour, incorporated into one of its new buildings in a depression that was once a fish pond, using Bin Brook which it now forms the mouth of, to supply it with water. Most of the college-owned punts are old Thames punts of traditional design, but as they become unsuitable for use, some have been replaced with Two Tees punts. The TT, or Two Tees, at Mathie's former yard in Chesterton, began building punts in 1970 and have built punts for Queens', Magdalene, Jesus, St John's, Wolfson and Darwin Colleges. Tyrrell and Tyler (TT) build punts distinctive for their high freeboard, the height of the sides above the water line, the design originating with the experience as Banham's employees. Two Tees punts are built for other rivers also and the high freeboard resists the wash of motor launches. Their punts are open at one end, with bottoms of marine ply, back rests screwed into the sides, cleats for strengthening, and decks resting on deck-beams. The length of their punts, indeed their ability to supply at all, depends on the availability of mahogany. Mahogany is not now usually supplied in lengths so long as 22ft.

In 1964, D.M. Reynolds, son of George Reynolds, appointed R.F. Bell as manager for Scudamore. Bell had previously been a merchant seaman, neither a waterman nor a boat builder. Reynolds had experimented unsatisfactorily with glass fibre craft. Bell began to think of designing a punt built on traditional lines, but planned for greatest suitability for the river; to fulfil these two requirements he was prepared to start with the function only in view. By 1967, Bell had developed a punt for his purpose and called the design the Camford punt. The frame was a box, not a ladder, and the punt was double-ended, with opposite ends identical. It was 21ft long and received its strength and rigidity from hardwood chines, holding the sides and bottoms together and from two very strong decks. The decks were designed to stand on and were supported by deck beams underneath them transversely, and by stringers fore-and-aft, the two together making a frame deliberately giving the deck the strength to fulfil the function of being stood on, the preference at Cambridge. Since the length of the punt was shortened, space for standing between the deck and the back rest was restricted further. There are battens along the sides, called cleats, looking like knees, to strengthen the sides and protect them from being stove in. The back rests forming the saloon were screwed into the sides, increasing rigidity. The bottoms were cross-planked. Each end was fitted with a chain and pin for mooring or tying up. Difficulty and damage were reduced when coming into or away from the landing stage because the punt was completely reversible, a useful consideration in the narrow Granta.

Both because there are no treads and because the decks and their supports are substantial and high, the centre of gravity of the Camford punt is high. It is smaller and lighter than a Thames punt and lacks comparable momentum. It is more delicate to handle and handles rather more like a canoe; its lightness and shortness makes it easier to steer. The Scudamore fleet of just over 100 punts now consists entirely of Camford punts. The boat builder at Scudamore is David Kitching, apprenticed at Banham. Scudamore's Boatyard also builds Camford punts for colleges and can quote for building them for private ownership. It buys mahogany by the log, for sawing up to order and seasoning, and can sometimes supply other boat builders with mahogany of 24ft–34ft lengths.

The standard of maintenance and service at Scudamore is high. A time-clock is used to check the hiring and return times. As with all punt-hirers, a substantial deposit is required, usually £15 or more. The punts at the three Scudamore landing stages and their equipment are kept in perfect order, ready for departure immediately, and the hirer is helped on his return. The poles are always well varnished and the cushions clean, tidy and in good repair.

Tyrrell, the other Cambridge punt-hirer, also builds similarly small punts, but more like a Thames punt than the Camford in that they are open at one end; some have one centre tread, with a chine as well; the bottom is marine ply. Tyrrell has about 20 punts at rafts at Quayside by Magdalene Bridge. Tyrrell also retail motor-craft; his yard is in Bermuda Road.

There are no aluminium punt poles at Cambridge. They have been tried but given up before their faults (blackening the hands;

bending under strain) were obviated, as at Oxford. Both punt-hirers at Cambridge supply only wooden poles; they are a little more expensive than aluminium poles (about £22, as against £18, without the shoes). They are not so durable as the heavy gauge aluminium poles used at Oxford. As elsewhere, the poles (of spruce) are supplied by F. Collar, of Oxford. Scudamore have experimented with laminated wood poles from Poland, but no advantage seems to have been derived from them.

The two places for hiring punts at Cambridge are Quayside and Granta Place. Quayside is below the Backs and Granta Place above them. Both Tyrrell and Scudamore have rafts with punts for hire at Quayside; only Scudamore has punts at Granta Place; with the weir there, the river at Granta Place is at two levels, so Scudamore hires separately for both from there. Between Granta Place and Quayside, the Backs are counted by many people as among the loveliest stretches of river in the country. The river passes along the backs of the colleges, through their gardens, past some of the finest buildings in England. With gardens the most attractive part of the river, it could be considered appropriate at Cambridge that the design of its pleasure punts, begun as Thames punts, should have reverted a little towards the indigenous garden punt... short, double-ended, box-framed and cross-planked.

Above the weir at Granta Place is the Granta. Because of the weir, the river is rather deeper and muddier than the Backs. The river is not wide. There are two and a half miles of river above the weir at Granta Place before the passage upwards is stopped by a weir at Byron's Pool. Beyond Grantchester, the river is so narrow in places that it can almost be jumped across. The usual goal of punters going upstream is Grantchester. At Grantchester, two miles upstream, are the Orchard Tea Rooms for tea and the Red Lion and Green Man for drinks and meals, both well arranged for receiving punting parties. Much of the

23

river is muddy with some holes in the river-bed giving extra depths; it passes through fields and open country. This is the countrified part of the river by contrast with the Backs which are gardens.

The entertainment of tourists and visitors in the Long Vacation has brought a recent proliferation of services supplied by punters. In 1975 the Conservators authorized J.M. Nicholson to provide punts with "chauffeurs"; the service has continued and a second, similar service has been added. More recently, punt parties are taken out and provided with strawberries and another enterprise, Picnic Punts, offers coffee, lunch, tea or cream tea in punts. Most of these entreprises are based either at the Anchor Hotel or at the bridge, both in Silver Street.

Though on a different river, the Great Ouse, there are two villages within reach of Cambridge, Hemingford Abbots and Hemingford Grey, which not only have punts for hire, but which have had an annual village regatta since 1904. From almost the start of it there were men's punting and ladies' punting events. In 1912, there was a dongola event; in 1922, punting in canoes and mixed doubles punting. It was not till 1951 that a cup, the Goodall Challenge Cup, was donated for men's punting, nor the Gaudin Cup for ladies' punting till 1979. The punts now used are ones built at Cambridge by Tyrrell. The organizers hope to introduce a double punting event once more. An unusual characteristic of punting in recent Hemingfords' Regattas has been the successful use of a "windmill" stroke, the pole being rotated, so that alternate ends touch the bottom.

R.C. Bending, a former T.P.C. amateur punting champion is now resident of a Hemingford and is teaching a more conventional and successful stroke. The "windmill" stroke is not comparably efficient. Hemingfords' Regatta claims to be the only remaining village regatta; organizers of Hurley and other regattas might disagree, but it may well be the best.

The punts for hire are at Houghton Mill, about a mile upstream from the Hemingfords. Most of the punts there are unusual in being only 14ft long, though able to seat four; there are also a few 21ft punts. Houghton Mill is at a lock and weir on the Great Ouse and the property of the National Trust; there has been a mill on the site since at least A.D. 974. Go through the mill to the tow-path beyond to reach the punt-hiring stage.

At one time punts were very popular on the Great Ouse, being found at Bedford, St Neots, Huntingdon, St Ives, Ely and other places. There is a boat builder, Granta Boats Ltd, at Ramsey on the River Nene in north Cambridgeshire, who builds 12ft, 14ft and 16ft punts of a design between a garden and a pleasure punt and of a small Thames-type punt, double-ended; they are all of marine ply, box-framed. The firm was founded at Cottenham fifty years ago and moved to Ramsey twenty-five years ago.

25

PER ARDUUM AD ALVEUM

Badge of the Cambridge University Dampers Club

Techniques of Punting

T HE FIRST PART of this chapter deals historically with the punting stroke, giving descriptions of it published between 1898 and 1960, with additions by R.C. Bending on training for punt racing and by Tony Christie on the bucket recovery. The second part deals with the stroke for beginners and for pleasure and racing punters, under different headings, and ends with advice on safety in punting and on the rule of the road; this part has been revised by, and includes a section by Penny Chuter, senior national rowing coach for Britain.

An early, but one of the most useful and thoughtful accounts of punting is given in Leslie's *Our River*. The more important parts of it are reproduced in Chapter 2. Though Leslie's was a fishing punt, his is the advice of an excellent waterman, and it deserves careful study by both experienced and inexperienced waterman.

In *Pleasure and Leisure Boating* (1899), Sydney Crossley includes a chapter on punting. His description is of running, not pricking a punt, and unlike other authors he has no interest in punt racing. He states three first principles for the learner: "I. Keep the pole parallel to the side, 2. Push in the exact opposite direction to that in which you want the punt to go, 3. Keep the pole out of the boat and your hands dry." Next he advises the beginner not to begin by using the pole, but to find a walled bank or some camp-shedding, to stand at the bow facing the stern, and to move the punt using the fingers. By this means, the learner will find how much effort is needed to change the direction of the punt and how it is applied with the fingers. The advice is excellent: for very little effort and change of direction is required to steer a punt, and movement of the fingers and forearms needed to move the punt along the wall is almost identical to their movement when using the pole. As a result the principle of punting with the fingers would be understood and experienced and established very early. Indeed, the pole planted parallel to the side might be considered as the wall, with a very slight angle in or out to steer. The fault of the novice, Crossley surmises, is to use too much effort: "He steps forward and makes a plunge with the iron (shoe)... His impetuosity is so great as nearly to send him over the side..." Crossley expects the punter to give constant thought to his task, and having written an earlier chapter on rowing, he concludes, "In point of science and recreation, punting beats rowing hollow." Like Leslie, he has a high regard for Maidenhead punts: "...all the best punts come from Maidenhead ... the best Maidenhead punts are shoved lighter, keep their 'way' better, hold themselves stiffer, and last longer than those built elsewhere." The punting stroke is described in each of the four books on punting and in later articles from journals or chapters from books. The first book on punting, *Rowing/Punting* (a double volume) by D.H. McLean & W.H. Grenfell (1898), is a reprint of Grenfell's article on punting in *The Suffolk Encyclopaedia of Sport* (1897/8). Grenfell gives good general advice on punting, Beesley's surname is misspelt throughout, though the coach is greatly praised by Grenfell, his pupil.

There are four photographs of Grenfell demonstrating the stroke, on dry land in a studio. His hands are at least 12in apart for the shove, and for the finish even more than this, perhaps from unfortunate posing. He includes a useful description of how to run a punt, giving it as the style of Edward Andrews; it is reprinted in Chapter 2, and its study is recommended to all interested in watermanship.

Grenfell's description of the stroke is as follows:

"A good punter should be able to punt either side equally well; but supposing that you are punting with the right hand leading, place your right foot firmly against a knee of the boat, or some other well-defined spot, where she balances the best, and keep it there. Fix your eyes on the bow of the punt right through the stroke, and do not let them come round with the pole, or you will lose your direction, and a punt should never be allowed to deviate a hairsbreadth from the true course. If the punt is going fast, drop in the pole well in front of you (the distance depends in a great degree on the depth of the river and the pace at which you are going), raise your hands as far up the pole as you can, get the weight well on, keeping the pole quite close to the chest, and finish with the weight on and the chest square. Then recover the pole smartly with the hands, draw the extended foot gently back, so as not to shake the punt, and commence the next stroke. The work should be done with the weight, loins, and legs, and not with the arms. In fact it is not unlike rowing. You reach forward to the full extent, apply the weight then take a step back which corresponds to sliding, finish square, and, as it were, slide slowly forward and repeat the dose. The long body swing, smart recovery with the hands, and slow sliding forward will always beat the snatchy armwork which is the pitfall of racing punts."

The second book, also *Rowing/Punting* (another double volume) by R.R.P. Rowe, C.M. Pitman & P.W. Squire (also 1898), was published in the Badminton Library of Sport. The author of Punting is P.W. Squire. He gives a full description of the stroke with the photographic illustrations of W. Haines, then professional champion. Whereas Grenfell's hands were at least a foot apart on the pole, Squire recommends six inches. His description is this:

"The pupil should practise punting on both sides; but we will assume that he will begin with his right leg forward, and will stand on the left side of the punt. The right foot should be placed in a position where it is not likely to slip; in light racing-punts special stops are fixed for the forward foot to rest against, but in the larger punts one of the 'knees' is used for this purpose."

"For starting a punt, the iron end of the pole is dropped in the water just behind the left foot, while the hands should grasp the pole rather higher up than the level of the punter's head, and the arms be extended well forward towards the head of the punt. In this position the pole will be as much slanted, and the punt should start as soon as the pull of the stroke begins. The reach of the left arm is much increased by bringing the left shoulder round and raising the left heel. Most of the weight of the body should be supported on the front or right leg, the balance of the body being assisted by the left leg resting on the toes of the left foot. The left shoulder is brought more round to get the catch at the beginning with the left hand, which is a very important feature of the punting stroke. In that position the right hand cannot reach the pole above the left, but it is held ready to catch on as soon as possible. There should be a space of about six inches between the hands, and as the punt moves forward the right hand can take up its proper position on the pole; the work is then done by both hands equally. The right knee is slightly bent, and this position assists the balance. When the pull has brought the hands to the body, the latter turns on the spine as an axis, and in the turn the stroke is completed by the sway of the body on to the left leg, and by pushing the hands away towards the stern of the punt. The left arm should finish about straight. The hands should pass with an even, uninterrupted motion, from the beginning of the stroke to the end, and the pressure on the pole should be continuous throughout. During the pull of the stroke the back foot travels over the floor of the punt, and comes to rest on it as the hands reach the body; the latter then turns, and when completing the stroke by pushing the arms out to their full extent, the left knee bends so as to allow the whole force to continue to the end. Without this bend of the knee the stroke is short and loses much of the power of what has been called the 'after shove' and 'back shove'.

"Picking up the pole in the recovery for the next stroke is by no means an unimportant part of punting. Immediately after the stroke is finished the right hand should draw the pole through the left to a certain distance, which will in each case depend upon the depth of the water and consequent length of the pole which has been used; the left hand will then throw the pole over the right, which in turn will catch it and the action will be completed by the right hand lifting the pole clear of the water in a vertical position, the left taking hold of it in its passage, and helping to support it until returned to the water. Having arrived at this position, the pole is not merely dropped into the water, but sent down sharply to avoid loss of time; it is allowed to pass freely through the left hand, which should at the same time be raised, bringing the left shoulder round to get as much reach forward as possible. This completes the description of the punting stroke as it should be practised."

B.H.B. Symons-Jeune published *The Art of Punting* privately in 1907, at the time when punting had reached its greatest popularity. The title of his book would be unacceptable today; for oarsmen, rowing is a technique, not an art, and so are the other skills of watermanship. Symons-Jeune stresses the importance of the stroke being made as a continuous action, and recommends counting to ensure there is no break in the swing. He describes the stroke thus, making three divisions for it:

"At the commencement of the stroke (Division I) the pole is sent down into the water with a rapid throw, in which the right hand passes the left, which at the same time is lifted upwards to grasp the pole in front of the body. The pole should strike the water well in front of the front foot according to the rate the punt is travelling: from three to four feet in a racing punt going down stream, to about six to eight inches in a heavy punt full of people going up stream. As the pole touches the bottom, the top of it is pointed well forward and upward and the centre cuts the water line about two inches behind the front foot. At this moment Division 2 commences by a pull begun by the left hand, while the right is passing upwards to assist in the stroke; as both hands come on to the pole they should be placed about two or three inches apart. It is a great mistake to have the hands too far apart, as it will interfere with the whole of the after-stroke. A very gentle play off the front toe will assist the punter to get his weight well on, and as this is applied the end of the pole should be slightly dropped, to allow the hands to pass across parallel and close to the chest, which swings round with the stroke. Meanwhile the hind foot should pass back over the floor of the punt as low as possible to it to a distance of two treads, or, in the case of a big man, two-and-a-half. If the step be longer than this it will be difficult to recover, and must jerk the punt. The back knee should be bent a little as it touches the ground, and when the pole comes round the weight is mainly transferred from the front leg to the back, which slowly pivots round on the ball of the foot until the toe points to the stern. The leg should move back in conjunction with the hands, but not before them, and as the hands reach the body they should be held close to the chest, while the latter swings round till it faces the stern. Up to this point the stroke has been a pull, and now it immerges gradually into a push. As the body turns round, both hands together should be thrust away with a push into which all the muscles of the chest as well as of the arms are put. It is this last extra shove which makes all the difference in the force of the stroke, for it occurs after the weight has been used, and when the punt is travelling at its fastest.

"As soon as the arms are extended to their fullest extent the recovery (Division 3 of the stroke) begins without the slightest pause. Both hands should draw in the pole until they are nearly level with the chest, and at that moment the back leg should swing up close to the front one and both should assume an erect position. The leg and the pole should swing up together as the motion of the former will lighten the exertion of lifting the pole, and ease the arms to a great degree.

"As to the motion of the hands in making the recovery, there are two ways; the first and usual way at present, though not the best is as follows. The pole after being drawn in slightly before the movement of the leg, is pulled by the right hand through the left and then brought forward by the left while the right hand presses underneath to hold it; this necessitates a change of hands and causes the weight of the pole to come more on the arms, which imparts a slight jerk between the throws of the pole from one hand to another.

"The modern way does away with this: the pole is passed from hand to hand by the right hand pulling it through the fingers of the left as far as is comfortable, when the left hand glides up the pole until close to the right, and so on until the pole is in an erect position; thus the hands never cross as in the previous method, and the pole is recovered in a much more slanting position and seems to swing up almost with the motion of the body."

Symons-Jeune recommends a distance of two to three inches between the hands on the pole. The recommended distance had been decreasing from Grenfell's to Squire's to Symons-Jeune's. In the modern racing stroke the hands are as close together on the pole as the hands on a golf club.

His description of the alternative or "modern" (as he calls it) method of picking up is interesting. The method was certainly not subsequently established in racing. It may have been a method of recovery seen used in Oxford for what is described later in this chapter as "punting with hands low." The conventional punting stroke was taught and used in Oxford; but in the 1890's there was certainly a style of punting, a vogue perhaps, possibly an Oxford idiosyncrasy, rather different in purpose, to achieve maximum relaxation, the body upright and making as little movement as possible. The idiosyncrasy may be of some historic interest. The technique perfected, it will be found no more difficult to punt sitting down than standing up (though that was not its purpose). I have taken the term "punting with hands low" from G.D. Leslie's advice to a novice learning to keep dry, "as soon as he learns to keep his hands low in working, the drips will no longer trouble him."

Symons-Jeune has a brief, useful chapter on steering; this advises against use of the swing: "A method often seen on the river for steering purposes is to take the end of the pole in both hands and swing it through the top of the water in either direction at the back of the punt... This is never to be recommended, and is never employed by good watermen to steer with, for it has several serious disadvantages." He then surmises obvious mechanical inefficiencies of it. He recognises the difference of effort required in steering a racing punt and a pleasure punt: "It is much easier to steer a racing punt and a two-foot than an ordinary punt, as the lightness of the vessel makes it answer much more quickly to every touch. Owing to the great weight of a heavy punt, it takes an effort to straighten it, and when once on the swing it is difficult to stop." He notes a change in style in the turning of the body: "A few years ago it was a golden rule never to take the eyes off the bow of the punt at any part of the stroke, as it enabled one to keep a straight course more easily. But now several expert punters turn their heads right round with their bodies; and there is no doubt that this enables them to get in a much longer back-shove with more strength to it."

Symons-Jeune's own interest was centred squarely in punt racing. He viewed pleasure punting perhaps with some disdain: "so many people think it is a sign of good punting to keep dry and not to splash the punt with water, and it is of course very useful for ladies punting for pleasure; but this can only be done by punting carefully and slowly, and it is absolutely impossible when travelling fast. In a race, for instance, everyone gets dripping, and very often an inch of water has to be baled out afterwards." He overstates the difficulty of keeping a punt dry when punting at pressure; for although in racing, a very fast recovery is a cause of wetness, it is possible in a pleasure punt to use a good deal of pace and pressure and to keep perfectly dry. Punting for pleasure, it was common at less pressure to use a comfortable and easy continuous half-shove.

Though an Oxford man, Symons-Jeune advised standing behind the after back-rest to punt, forward of the till: "When carrying passengers, the punter should stand in the stern of the punt with his front foot placed against the 'knee' of the punt, just behind the back of the seat. This will allow him room enough to step well back in his stroke, whereas if he stands in the bows, the slope of the punt will render his position less secure." There is, in fact, no difference of slope for either position when standing immediately behind a back-rest, whether punting bow first or stern first (from the Oxford end). Perhaps he wished to emphasise the orthodoxy on the Thames of punting bow first. There would of course have been no question of standing on the till; it would have been regarded as a misuse of the punt.

An article in *Every Woman's Encyclopaedia* (about 1908 – the British Library catalogue does not have it) gives advice for punting. Some of it is taken verbatim from Squire and Grenfell, well selected and arranged in numbered items. "It is very important to acquire a good style in punting from the outset, for when once this is fixed, it is almost impossible to alter it... I. when punting alone in the boat, stand almost in the middle of the punt, close to the right hand side, in order to make a slight keel by means of your weight. 2. Punt on the right-hand side of the boat, at least while learning, because this enables you to get the first pull on the pole with the right hand and arm — almost always considerably stronger in a woman — and when the art of punting on that side has been mastered, by all means practise punting from the left-hand side also, for to be able to punt from either side is often a great advantage, especially for punt racing at regattas. 3. Keep the hands quite close to each other on the pole, and never move them from their first position throughout the stroke. When turning the punt, the hands are placed a couple of feet apart, instead of within about six inches of each other. 4. *Steer entirely by means of the pole on the bottom of the river.* Never steer with the pole in the water behind the boat as though it were a rudder. 5. Pick up the pole with three clean-cut movements, never draw it up hand over hand. 6. Return the pole to the water with a single throw." The instructions are well expressed; but right-handed punt racers prefer to stand on the left side.

There are good descriptions of the punting stroke in *Punting* by A.M. Winstanley (1922). He gives a long and detailed description of the stroke and concludes with the brief summary quoted later; this summary is as useful as his longer description. The introduction to Winstanley's *Punting* (1922) was written by Lord Desborough (W.H. Grenfell). In this introduction, Lord Desborough described the punting stroke briefly and very effectively understood by any oarsman. He compared it, as other writers had done, to the rowing stroke: "In punting, as in rowing, you should (1) come slowly forward with the body; (2) reach well up the pole and get your weight on to the beginning; (3) swing well back, using the free leg like a sliding seat; (4) finish the stroke well out, turning the body from the hips, but not letting it tumble forward; (5) recover the pole sharply with the hands; and (6) slide, as it were, slowly forward again by bringing up the disengaged leg without shaking the punt."

In 1926, in *The Civil Service Sports Journal*, A.E. Banham wrote an article on punting. His description of the punting stroke, except for the pick up or recovery, is very lucid: "Stand at the side of the punt, not facing forward, but with the shoulders just about 'square', i.e., parallel, to the river bank. The head only should be turned forward. We will suppose that the punter is standing on the left side of the punt, as one looks forward. The left hand at the height of the waist holds the pole in an almost vertical position. The right hand at a height a little above the head steadies the pole. The pole is then thrown down smartly with the right hand so that its shoe rests on the bottom of the river, the left hand comes up to the full extent of the arm and catches the pole, the weight of the body is hung on the pole and the right hand comes up and grips the pole above and touching the left. The stroke has now commenced. The pull on the pole by means of the arms changes smoothly into a push as the hands pass exactly across the middle of the chest and the right shoulder comes on to the work. The stroke is carried right through and finishes with hands well behind. It is the last part of the stroke – known as the backshove – that the untrained punter usually omits... The pectoral muscles have to be developed a bit by practice if the stroke is to pass in one strong unbroken movement from the natural pull with which it commences into a rearward shove." Banham adds, "Don't stand on the counter (or deck) of the punt. It is impossible to punt properly there, and none of the real punting fraternity ever does it."

Banham gives advice on steering: "When the beginner comes to steer he should remember that steering should not be done by trailing the pole behind and using it as a rudder. This spoils poles and wastes time. Steering is all done in the stroke and it is done thus. To steer to the left, simply draw the hands inboard a little during the latter part of the shove, the pole being levered against the side of the punt ... it is obvious that if you lever or 'pinch' the after-end to the right, the fore-end will swing to the left.

"Steering to the right is as difficult to learn as steering to the left is easy... get the punt moving and during the latter part of the stroke lean out and bring the punt towards the pole by a combined use of the arms, weight and (in imagination perhaps) toes."

He concludes with a succinct description of racing, "A punting race finishes where it starts and usually consists of ¼ mile each way, the turning point being marked by poles standing up in the river, known as 'ryepecks'. A punt is reversible like a tramcar, and the turn is accomplished by dropping the pole far forward, bringing the punt to a dead stop, and steering the stern which has now become the bow, round the ryepeck as the punt starts on the return journey... Punt races start downstream, the turn is toward the bank and the finish is, of course, up-stream." It is more usual to recommend the steering for the turn as the punt first passes the ryepeck, passing from one side to the other behind the pole before the stop-up is made; the turn is then completed as the stop-up finishes, and the punt is pointing straight forwards towards to the finish as it repasses the ryepeck coming up-stream. Punt races are almost always started downstream because the direction of the stream holds them straighter for the start than if started upstream. The course usually taken is the midstream side going downstream, to use the current, and the bank-side to avoid it coming up; therefore the turn is usually made towards the bank. Punters on the whole prefer to make the turn against the stream, from downstream to upstream.

In 1929, Giles gave instructions on the menu card for Lyons tea shops as do's and don'ts. Among his do's and don'ts he said: "Do not try to use a long, heavy pole — a 13ft pole is quite long enough for most reaches on the Thames. It should not be so big that you cannot get your hand comfortably around it. If you want to improve your punting, go out alone and stand in the middle of the punt. In that position, you will be far less affected by cross-winds and much less likely to oversteer. Do not try to steer by waving the pole about in the water behind the punt. When steering is necessary, put the pole into the water, sloping either towards you or away from you and either push the punt slightly away or pull it towards the pole as you push the punt along. "Do not stand on the counter or decked-in part at the stern of the punt. Apart from being quite incorrect, this is one of the most difficult places from which to punt. Always make sure that the pole has touched the bottom of the river before you push on it. This may sound silly, but carelessness in this respect is the usual cause of people falling in. If your pole sticks in the mud, it is far safer to let go, and then paddle back and fetch it. If you try to hang on, it will probably pull you into the water." The Thames Punting Club regatta programme for 1949 included a short article on punting. For the punting stroke, it gave the following advice.

"The first golden rule of punting is, *Never move the foot nearest the bow.* It should be securely wedged against one of the 'knees', with the foot at an angle of approximately 60 degrees to the side of the punt. (The knees are the small wooden struts fastened along each side.) "Next in importance is always, at the commencement of each new stroke, to stand erect, with heels together, and body and head facing forward. Reach high up the pole with the rear hand, and immediately the pole has touched the bed of the river place the other hand just above, grasp firmly with both hands, lean forward, slope the top of the pole slightly down to the bow, pull down and shove across the chest.

"Remember to keep head facing in the direction the boat is going — it is not until the top of the pole is level with the punter that he should swing round on his hips and face sideways. Meanwhile, the forward foot remains stationary, takes the whole weight of the body and is pressed forcibly against the bottom of the boat. The rear foot should now be raised an inch and gently slid along the bottom and side of the punt towards the stern. When the punter faces sideways, but not before, the rear foot is brought firmly to rest on the bottom of the boat and the weight is transferred to that foot.

"During the whole of the stroke the forward foot never moves, and the two hands must maintain exactly the same position on the pole. Never allow the hands to be parted whilst putting weight or pressure on the pole. A continuous even pressure should be applied and maintained throughout the stroke until the body has turned so far round that the pole is touching the forward shoulder. At the completion of the stroke, the forward hand draws — or gently swings — the pole up through the rear hand, the rear hand forming a loose ring round the pole. Avoid splashing. At the same time the rear foot should be brought up to the forward one. See that all your actions are smooth: care must be taken not to 'rock' the boat.

"Whereas the bow and the stern should be approximately at the same level, it is a mistake to think that a punt must lie flat on the water. It should tilt along its whole length towards the side on which the punter stands. If, therefore, a passenger occupies the centre, that passenger should be at the opposite end, but on the same side, as the punter. Friction with the water will be minimised, and consequently less effort required to propel the punt.

"By sloping the pole, whilst it is on the bottom of the river, towards or away from the punt you either push the stern away from or draw it towards the pole, thus steering the punt in the required direction. Never try to lever the punt over against the pole: more poles are broken in this way than through any other cause. No punter should stand on the rear deck: punting should be performed from the well of the punt."

In 1953, Nevill Miroy wrote an article on punting for *The Light Blue*, a Cambridge sports magazine. His advice for the punting stroke was, "The would-be punter should take up his position about three-quarters of the way towards the stern of the craft on the port or starboard side, and let the pole slide through his hands until it just touches the bottom. The angle at which he starts this movement is judged so as to bring the underwater end of the pole just astern of him as it touches the bottom; therefore when the 'shove' is started, the pole is approximately at an angle of 45° to the bottom and to the punter. If his craft has 'way on', the punter thrusts the pole well forward to allow time for it to reach the bottom. He then thrusts astern with both arms, taking a step in the same direction with the rear foot. At the end of a stroke, he pulls the pole forward almost horizontally above the water, either gathering it in hand over hand, or by a sharp jerk throwing it forward so that it slides through his fingers. As it comes up, the lower end is brought forward ready to re-enter the water at the correct angle, and at the same moment the feet are brought neatly together.

"*Steering is probably the most difficult part of punting.* If a punter wants to steer his craft to the left while punting on the right, he puts his pole into the water a foot or so from the side of the boat, and, while making his stroke, draws the stern of the punt towards the pole, even allowing the pole to go slightly underneath the stern; but he must take care not to get the pole under the boat or he may be pulled out. If he wants to steer to the right, then during the stroke he pushes the stern slightly away from the pole. It is important not to get a 'swing' on the boat as this is difficult to stop."

In 1960, the EP Publishing Group added to its series of booklets on sports the title *Know the Game: Boating,* now out of print. It had three sections: on sculling, canoeing and punting. The section on punting was written by R.C. Bending, T.P.C. champion from 1946–49. As a keen amateur photographer, Bending took photographs of punting for it; an artist then made line drawings of them for the illustrations in the book. For a punter standing on the left of the punt, his instructions for the stroke were: "Stand in the punt with your right foot close to the side and at an angle of 45°. Face square forward and hold the pole with your right hand at the distance of your own height from the shoe of the pole; your left hand holds it loosely about three feet below. Throw the pole down with your right hand and follow it down letting it slide through your fingers. Simultaneously reach well up and forward with your left hand and as soon as the pole hits the bottom, grip it with your left hand and start to pull. As soon as you start to pull with your left hand, reach up with your other hand and grip the pole above the left hand. Your rear foot will automatically lift a little as your right hand reaches up. Pull both hands in towards your chest and at the same time slide your rear foot backwards about two feet, depending on the length of your leg and the amount of effort being put into the stroke. Your front knee may bend slightly and the weight of your body should come on to the pole. Now turn your trunk round and begin to bend your rear knee. Continue to swing your trunk round, at the same time shooting your hands out towards the rear, and continue to bend your rear knee in a lunging movement. The recovery can be done in a leisurely manner. Grip the pole with your right hand and pull it through the left hand, at the same time turning your trunk towards the front. When punting in deep water it is advisable to spread your arms well out. Then grip the pole with your left hand and continue to move it up. Move your right hand backwards down the pole and grip it at a point about your own height from the bottom. (For punting with a long pole in deep water it may be necessary to repeat the movements to bring the pole clear of the water.)" By this Bending is advising a pick up in five: the pick up should always be made in an odd number of movements, whether in one – the bucket – or in three, or in more. "Move your right hand, which is now gripping the pole, up and forwards and continue to swing your body round towards the front. Draw the pole through your left hand until your hands are about three feet apart. Your weight will now be over your front foot and the other foot is drawn smoothly towards it. At the same time bring the pole towards the upright position. Continue to move your body round until it is facing square forward and bring the pole ready into the first position." His special advice on steering is: "Only steer *half* the angle you wish to turn, the swing of the punt will look after the rest."

Bending's instructions do not seem to make clear enough the importance of the control of the pole with the rear hand of the forward and lateral angles as it moves to the upright position for the drop when he says, "the left hand holds it (the pole) loosely": the hand should be relaxed, but its movement and control at this point decide precisely the place and angle for the drop of the pole. Bending's instructions were based on his racing stroke with modifications to reduce its pressure for pleasure punting. Bending, regarded as an exceptionally good stylist, said however that when racing he punted standing virtually on one foot. Though the rear foot moved back and forward for the after-shove, it hardly touched the punt; the body recovered its position at the end of the shove from its weight on the pole, not the foot. That Bending appeared to stand only on one foot when racing is confirmed by those who watched him.

Notes provided by R.C. Bending on training for punt racing include this advice: "I. Get a good coach. 2. Develop a good style. 3. Do most of your long distance early in the season so that your style gets well established. 4. Get out in all conditions. Learn to handle the punt when a half gale is blowing. 5. Get to know the course. 6. Never waste time at the ryepeck. When turning move across the ryepeck as you pass it, so that when you stop up and reverse, your course is then directly ahead. Pass as closely as possible. 7. Practise dropping the pole and picking up the spare without losing rhythm. Picking up the pole on the same side can be done without any check, but also practise picking up the pole on the opposite side without a check. 8. Follow down the throw with the hand. This will cope with any pot holes. 9. Do not use a pole longer than necessary for the course."

Punt racers have always believed that a large proportion of races are won or lost at ryepecks. A punter picks up the spare pole with almost the same movement as the recovery, moving lower for it, so to the unobservant watcher a pole left behind may appear in the river as if from nowhere; with the hands relaxing at the end of the stroke, a pole sticking is left by the momentum of the punt.

This description of the bucket recovery is provided by Tony Christie, T.P.C. champion for 1961–3. "The shove through the water right up to the finish of the stroke is the normal power transmission. It is at the point of recovery that the variation arises. The forward hand draws the pole through the rear hand and the body turns towards the bow, both in one movement. The rear hand checks its forward momentum as the forward hand raises the pole ready for the downward throw for the next stroke. The forward hand throws the pole down, and the rear hand now above head height checks the pole as it strikes the bottom, holding it momentarily as the forward hand reaches above the rear hand and the stroke begins. The bucket, a forward movement in one, is far the fastest recovery, comparable to the hands away and forward movement on the slide of a best and best sculling boat." By comparison with the stroke with the pick up in three, the finish for the stroke with the bucket recovery is often made high, the stroke shorter and with a higher striking rate. Among racing punters in 1982, there is a tendency not to move the rear foot, which mechanically cannot be so efficient as when the foot is moved well to give a longer stroke. Before the introduction of the bucket, the word "throw" was always used for second movement of the recovery in the pick up in three, the forward throw of the pole by the rear hand. In modern punt racing, with the pick up in one, the word "throw" is not needed in describing the recovery, and it is often used now to describe what was formerly called the drop, the throw of the pole with the forward hand down to the river-bottom.

The side preference in punting is estimated at about 60–65% on the left and 35–30% on the right. Punters should learn on both sides early, because if one side only is learnt in the early stages it is very difficult to learn on the other side.

The foregoing descriptions of the punting stroke provide a historical account of it. The following descriptions are for those immediately concerned with the practice of punting.

Paddling a Punt with Canoe Paddles

Paddling a punt is a pleasant alternative to punting it, with either double paddles or single. Using two paddles, the paddlers sit side by side on the till, with a back-rest cushion for a seat. Steering is done by increasing or reducing pressure on one side or the other. For paddling a punt with a single paddle, the stroke has technical similarities to the punting stroke. A racing punt carries no paddle, and if it must be paddled, it is done with the pole.

Paddling a Punt with a Pole or Paddle

The stroke for a single paddle in a punt is the same as the stroke in a Canadian canoe.

A description of the stroke for the Canadian canoe follows, but a comparison with the punting stroke is included with it. It is even more relevant than the comparison with the rowing stroke. The difference, as with rowing, is that the paddle is forced against the water and the pole against the river bottom. Anyone who is competent in using a single canoe paddle and has not punted, will soon find himself able to punt after a short distance, if he will first propel the punt using the pole with the stroke of a single canoe paddle. The steering of a canoe with a paddle and a punt with a pole is almost identical.

To steer a canoe with a single paddle away from the side the paddler is paddling on, dip the paddle into the water (at a right angle to the side) a little away from the canoe; then towards the end of the stroke, turn the blade inwards, pulling it in towards the canoe. This effectively draws the stern towards the paddle and thus turns the bow away. To steer towards the side the paddler is paddling on, put the paddle in close to the canoe; then towards the end of the stroke, turn the blade outwards, pushing it away from the canoe (or if the blade is well under the canoe, lever it against the side). This is called the "J" stroke by canoeists and in effect it levers the stern away from the paddle, effectively turning the bow towards the "paddling" side. So also when a punt is steered from anywhere astern of the centre, direction is changed by pushing the stern, not the bow, away from or towards the pole. When running a punt from the bow, it is of course the direction of the bow that must be changed. The mechanics of steering a punt are exactly the same as steering a canoe, except that the pole is first thrown (or dropped) to the bottom. The former movement is the equivalent of "shoving around" and the latter of "pinching" the punt; a canoe was once also said to be "pinched".

If the experienced canoeist, while standing, learns to paddle with the lower part of the punt pole and steers as if with a single canoe paddle, he can then progress by throwing the pole down instead of dipping it, and will find he begins punting with the proper mechanical technique almost immediately, based on the single paddle stroke.

A pleasure punter should be able to paddle well with his pole; it is necessary in deep water and very useful over mud, so he should learn and practise it. Besides using a pole like a single canoe paddle, a punter, standing, can hold the pole horizontally across the punt like a double (kayak) canoe paddle, to paddle, dipping on alternate sides. Though requiring more effort than punting, a good speed can be maintained with either stroke when the punt has momentum.

Always take a canoe paddle in a punt in case you drop the pole and need to recover it. Some punt-hirers now provide paddles too small to allow good paddling. Ask for a large paddle if you intend to use it for more than this.

A competent punter with good balance may find enjoyment in punting a Canadian canoe. It can also be useful practice for punt racing. Lacking the weight of a punt, however, its movement will also lack the smoothness and momentum of a punt. Some regattas have canoe punting races. The major trophy is the Dardier Cup at the Sunbury Regatta.

The Punting Stroke

Skill in rowing or punting is the achievement of maximum mechanical efficiency from physical effort; of maximum physical effort for full pressure and of minimum for light pressure. Pressure is determined by the length of stroke as well as by physical effort. In punting at full pressure, the pole comes to the vertical and if the punt is in deep water will be dropped ahead of the punter's forward foot. The full shove consists of two parts; the first, a pull on the pole as the hands are drawn towards the centre of the chest, the second a push when the hands pass it. The rear foot moves back with the push, to complete the "after shove" and comes forward again with the recovery. In punting, length of stroke can be reduced by using a "half-shove", dropping the pole at half the angle to the vertical, or 45°; or a ¾-shove, using three-quarters of the angle. When a punt is stationary or moving very slowly, it is necessary to use a half-shove to start it moving. A pleasure punt is heavy and its movement requires momentum. Until this is established, it is better to use half or three-quarter shoves, usually for the first three strokes.

A good punter should be able to punt from either side of the punt at any point along it from bow to stern. For racing, the forward foot is placed at, or just forward of, the centre point of the side against a "knee", and does not move from that position; also in a pleasure punt, but only as far forward as the saloon will allow. The nearer to the centre the punter stands, the less physical effort and movement required for steering during the stroke. In a pleasure punt, therefore, the punter should stand as far forward as the design of the punt allows. A racing punt is easier to steer than a pleasure punt, being lighter. If a beginner in a pleasure punt is improving and can take the opportunity to remove the saloon cushions and punt from there, it will assist in learning to steer during the stroke. A right-handed punt racer often prefers to stand on the left of the punt, so his right hand and foot are forward to begin the pull of the shove, the moment of greatest effort.

The punt will steer better if as much weight as possible, including that of the "sitters" or sitting passengers, is kept on the same side of the punt as the punter, thereby tilting the punt towards that side. This makes a shallow keel, helping to keep the punt straight. Both feet should be kept as near to the side as possible, with the forward foot pointing at an angle slightly forward and remaining stationary through-out the stroke.

In punting, the matter of greatest importance is posture. Almost every mistake follows from incorrect posture. The body must be relaxed and upright. Any bending of the back or crouching will cause inefficiency and possibly danger. Punting is a posture exercise, like rock-climbing, dancing or golf. Muscle tension of the rest of the body should never exceed that of the fingers. To maintain this rule may be a difficult discipline for a beginner, but it should be learnt. It is for this reason that with the stroke at fullest pressure, the hands cross the front of the chest as close to it as possible, while the body is relaxed and absolutely upright as the forward knee begins to bend.

The first and most important rule in punting therefore is to relax and keep upright. The beginner may feel that this is absurd, because thereby much less effort than is expected may be required, and the discovery may nonplus a beginner. However, keep two questions in mind. Can I stand even more upright? Can I make even more use of my fingers? When thinking about the movements of the stroke, keep your thoughts on the movement of your fingers; relaxing the rest of your, muscles, the rest of your movements will follow correctly. Stand upright and relax.

Some Descriptions of the Punting Stroke

Four descriptions of punting follow for different stages of progress; first, for an absolute beginner lacking confidence; second, for the improver with pleasure punting in mind; third, for the beginner confident in handling a punt pole of any weight; finally a description by A.M. Winstanley of the old racing stroke with the recovery (or pick up) in three, before the introduction of the very light aluminium racing pole which made the pick up in one (the "bucket") the general practice in punt racing. One of the greatest stylists since the introduction of the bucket, punted in best and best punts virtually standing on only one foot all the time.

For the Absolute Beginner

The absolute beginner is recommended to:

I. Stand near the end of the punt. If punting stern first, as at Oxford, stand at the top of the slope, or "swim"; if bow first, as at Cambridge, on the deck. If your balance is poor, you may stand with one foot away from the side; but as you gain confidence, be sure to bring it back to the side. Standing with one foot away from the side is less efficient mechanically and more dangerous when in difficulty. Many beginners do it, standing diagonally to the side because they feel safer. The stance becomes a habit and the faulty style is then difficult to change.

2. Use ½ or ¾ shoves, with ¾ as the maximum. This means, do not bring the pole upright. Throw it backwards and down with the forward hand, parallel and close to the side, with the lower hand to guide it, not to grip it. Do not check the pole when you have let it drop. It must fall uninterrupted all the way. Do not try to push it to the bottom, hand over hand. Wait until it touches. If it doesn't reach the bottom, recover it and try another half shove.

3. When the pole has reached the bottom, reach forward and pull the pole gently past your chest. The harder you pull, the more serious your steering errors will be.

4. When you have reached the end of your shove, relax your arms and the grip of your hands on the pole. (It is very important to develop this as a habit, because it ensures you do not fall in if the pole unexpectedly sticks.) Let the pole float to the surface, use it like a rudder, swinging it to one side or the other. Some beginners inexperienced in boats have difficulty in steering: the pole must be swung to the same side as the direction in which you wish to travel.

5. Recover the pole hand to hand until you can begin to tilt it. When it can tilt, tilt it half way and begin another half-shove. An absolute beginner may be helped by a passenger using a paddle, especially to help steer, but as little help as possible should be given, or the punter will not learn.

For the Improver in a Pleasure Punt

The Recovery

Much of the wetness to clothes and to punts is caused by not keeping the hands and pole over the water and by gripping the pole too hard when recovering. The punt is a heavy craft and once it is moving the momentum will carry it for the distance given by two or three shoves. Therefore it is not necessary to recover early if you are not racing. The momentum of a punt is sufficient to pull a pole out of the bottom (except in mud, which you should be paddling over with your pole). It is unnecessary therefore to pull the pole out of the bottom. The pole is able to float of its own accord; it is unnecessary therefore to try to lift it or pull it from the water. Wait for it to float. If the pole is unvarnished and rough, allow time for water to run off it. You can hold the pole, floating astern with one finger of the forward hand if you wish; you can adjust the steering with a swing, if you wish, with a finger of the rear hand; no more effort is usually required, except in wind or a cross-stream. If you are punting for pleasure, this is another position in which to check your posture; relax and stand upright, with arms and hands low. Take a few moments to look at the river, to rest and to enjoy it.

The recovery should be made in an odd number of movements. The pick up in three is the usual. If you cannot pick up in three, pick up in five (or even seven). If you pick up in an even number, the control for angle will not come into the correct, the rear, hand, before the beginning of the next stroke. If you have an opportunity to use a pole on dry land, you can practise the pick up in three on a concrete, wood or gravel surface. It is a good movement to practise in this way because you can also ensure that you relax and keep upright at the same time. For the pick up in three, the forward hand, with an underhand grip, draws the pole forward. As it reaches its limit, the rear hand grips it overhand and throws it on. The forward hand grips it below and moves it forward to begin the tilt. The rear hand following below, forces the pole down and thereby moves it up to the vertical against the pressure from the now rigid forward arm. The rhythm of the pick up in three is long-short-long, and the sequence of movement is pole-body-foot.

The Drop or Throw
At the end of the recovery with the pole upright, the rear hand controls two nearly vertical angles; first, the angle of the tilt, forward or back, parallel to the side of the punt, altered for the depth of the water or the length of the stroke; secondly, the angle of the tilt sideways, used in steering. Both hands control the distance of the pole from the side. Concentrate on the control of the pole by the rear hand and perfect this. If the movement is not going well, keep the forward hand low. The lower the hands, the greater the control over the pole. If you are having difficulty dropping the pole at the right angle and place, keep the grip on the pole with the rear hand, held as low as possible, and use the forward hand to hold the pole lightly. When its position is correct, let the pole drop from the rear hand, following it with a light flick from the fingers of the forward hand or letting it slide through them. Do this until you have learnt control with the lower hand. Never check the fall of a pole. If it does not fall as you want, learn to control its position, concentrating on the use of the rear hand. Do not try to control its tilt forwards or sideways with the forward hand. Keep your fingers relaxed enough to feel the nature of the vibration as the pole strikes the bottom; it will always vary slightly and may tell you how to make your shove.

When the control of the pole has been mastered, so that it can be guided with perfect accuracy, it can be thrown with maximum effort by the forward hand (provided the river bottom is suitable). Penny Chuter describes the movement thus: "The correct movement should be compared with throwing a javelin, i.e., the arm is held straight behind the thrower and the power and trajectory of the javelin comes from the arm throwing from straight behind and across the body to straight in front and above the head; similarly, the pole is thrown directly into the water from reaching straight above the head until the arm is straight downwards."

When you are stationary, or moving slowly, remember that the pole must go into the water at an angle backwards. If you are stationary in shallow water, the angle should be at least 45°. This is called a half-shove. If you are moving slowly, the angle can be less. Establishing momentum in a pleasure punt usually requires three half-shoves.

The Shove

Tighten your fingers enough at the beginning of the shove to make sure the shoe is firmly fixed in the river-bottom. This is the moment to check your posture; relax, straighten your body and as you begin to pull, for the first part of the shove, come to your most upright position with your body at its fullest height, drawing your hands towards you. This brings your hands close across the front of your chest. Turn and push away. Move your rear foot back, but do not bring your hands any lower than the descent made necessary by moving the foot. The back should be straight and the head up. If you are not certain of your direction or steering, resist putting weight on the beginning of the shove. Direction can be changed over the first foot or two of the shove, but not if you have shoved too hard and are travelling fast. At the end of the shove, the hands and fingers relax on the pole, if only momentarily. It is important to establish this relaxation as an unvarying habit. Again, when the fingers tighten to recover the pole, the tension, by habit, should never be so great as to pull the body backwards if the pole sticks. Leaving the pole behind if it has stuck too hard should be a reflex action. For the racing stroke, it is common to see the fingers stretch out on the pole before the recovery.

Steering

Steering is part of the shove. The punt is steered by the angle at which the pole is thrown down. To steer away from the side you are facing, drop the pole so that its bottom is just outside the vertical line from the side of the punt to the river bottom and the top is a little further out still, making an inward slope with the pole a little away from the punt. Keeping as upright as possible, in spite of having to reach out, pull in towards you during the shove. This is "shoving around". To steer towards the side you are facing, throw down the pole close to the side you are facing and lean the pole inwards, so the top of the pole passes slightly over the side of the punt. This is called "pinching" the punt. With the precisely correct angle, the shove is made with both hands close together and the pole finishing straight astern.

With a heavy punt or a strong cross wind, when more strength is required, more leverage for steering can be obtained, using the same mechanical principle, by spreading the hands apart a little, usually by lowering the grip of the rear hand; then pushing outwards or pulling inwards with the lower hand during the stroke to move the stern towards you or away from you as you continue the shove, you will steer towards or away from the bank facing you. To steer away from the bank facing you ("shoving around"), the pole must be dropped well away from the side and pulled inwards. The wider apart the hands are, the more powerful will be the movement in steering.

The mechanical principle used in steering is to push the stern away or draw it in with the pole during the stroke. Using short sideways strokes of this kind, you can turn the punt in a complete circle either way without moving it forwards or backwards.

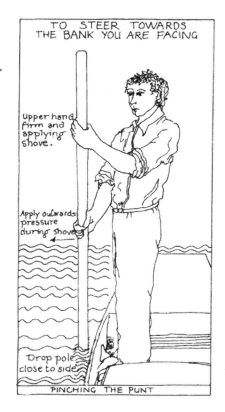

TO STEER TOWARDS
THE BANK YOU ARE FACING

Upper hand
firm and
applying
shove.

Apply outwards
pressure
during shove

Drop pole
close to side

PINCHING THE PUNT

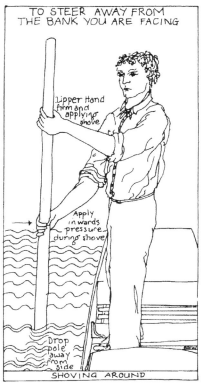

TO STEER AWAY FROM
THE BANK YOU ARE FACING

Upper Hand
firm and
applying
shove

Apply
inwards
pressure
during shove

Drop
pole
away
from
side

SHOVING AROUND

Steering under difficulty. When the pole is dropped with the correctly chosen lateral angle, no more need be done during the shove to move in the chosen direction. However, a reserve of mechanical force in steering a heavy punt in a cross-wind or in turning a sharp corner may be obtained by lowering the grip of the rear hand on the pole and pulling in or pushing out with it while making the shove, drawing the stern of the punt towards or pushing it away from the pole, thus turning the bow in the other direction. For "shoving around", forward pressure of the waist, knees and toes draws the stern of the punt towards the pole. For "pinching", the stern may be touched with the pole to turn it, but that is by no means essential.

For the Beginner Confident in Handling a Punt Pole

This description of the punting stroke by Penny Chuter is valuable for beginners who are confident in handling a punt pole.

The Recovery

Start with the pole "trailing" in the water at the end of a stroke with hands together on the pole.

The forward hand (under-hand grip) is nearest the top of the pole with the rear (over-hand grip) next to the forward hand and touching it. The pole is recovered by working the hands down hand-over-hand as follows. Grip pole with forward hand and pull it with forward hand up and across body with the rear hand holding loosely, and allow pole to be pulled through rear-hand fingers with right hand. When forward hand ahead of body, grip with the rear hand to stop pole moving and whilst gripping with rear hand, move the forward hand down pole crossing below rear hand. Then grip and support pole in forward hand and move rear hand down pole as far as possible. (If this "crossover recovery" does not get your hands far enough down the pole, then repeat the movement by crossing the forward hand below the rear hand again, etc.)

The hands will now be apart and ready to carry the pole forward for the next stroke. As the pole is moved forward and vertical, the rear foot also moves up closer to the forward foot.

The Beginning (The Throw)

Just before the beginning, the weight is on the forward foot and the pole is held vertically in front of the body with the forward hand above the head and the rear hand holding it at about waist level. The pole is then thrown towards the bottom with the top (forward) hand throwing down and guiding the direction of the pole whilst simultaneously the lower hand is taken off the pole and moved up to grip the pole at maximum reach above the head. This hand immediately begins to pull as the forward hand, having thrown the pole down, then reaches up to grip the pole above (and touching) the other hand so that both are together on the pole. During the stroke the hands must be together on the pole (touching) so that the "reach" and "back-shove" equally share the pressure.

Normally the pole is thrown in vertically about 1 ft in front of the forward foot. If the water is deep, it should be angled about 20° forward. If very shallow, about 10° backwards.

The Stroke

As both hands, and arms and shoulders, begin to pull downwards and towards the body, the rear foot steps back. As the hands are drawn across the body, the full weight is on the forward foot and the pole. As the hands pass across the body, the upper body turns with the pole and a strong back-shove is executed with the forward shoulder. As this is done, some body weight is transferred to the rear foot.

Remember the whole stroke is executed with hands together on the pole.

You are now ready to start the recovery again.

Practise the recovery movement with a broomstick at home or with a punt pole, standing on the bank. This will make your first effort afloat easier.

Steering

Steering may be done in two ways:

A straight shove and steer with the pole.

A "C" shaped shove from out, to in, to out, to "pinch" the punt (or move to the pole-side of the punt); and a "C" shaped shove from in, to out, to in, to "shove around" (or move away from the pole-side).

The Stroke at Full Pressure

Winstanley won the first Thames Punting Championship held after the 1914–1918 war. After a long description in his book of the punting stroke, he ends with a neat summary of it, reminiscent of the style of an army training manual, calling it "punting by numbers". (For everyday English, replace his full stops with "and" as appropriate.) He describes the stance, with the assumption that the left side is chosen when facing the bow: "The toes of the right foot should be against one of the 'knees' of the punt, and should never move from that position. The foot should form an angle with the side of the punt and not be straight across at right angles. The position of the left foot at the commencement of the stroke is close up to the right foot, and straight across the punt. The body should be upright but not stiff, and should be free on the hips and well balanced on the ankles. It is good practice in balancing, to stand in the position decribed and rock the punt by means of the ankles only."

Winstanley divides the stroke into lifting and dropping the pole:

"Lifting Pole. Left hand resting on pole, right hand underneath, feet together, right foot against a 'knee'. Hands close to side. (1) Right arm rises to the horizontal, right hand gripping pole. Left hand acts as slide. (2) Left hand grips pole. Right hand slides down pole until close to left. (3) Drop pole from left hand to right. (4) Right arm rises until is level with forehead and just in front of it, right hand gripping pole. Left hand reaches down pole, grips it and pushes it forward.

"Dropping Pole. (The Throw) (5) Pole allowed to drop while left hand slides up it to *full extent of arm*. Right hand follows pole down, fingers touching pole, until arm is extended fully downwards. Left hand must be well round pole. (6) When pole touches bottom, right hand raised and grips pole just above left hand. (7) Arms and body reach forward to give maximum angle on pole, at the same time left leg raised and moved back, foot not touching bottom. (8) Draw hands in towards chest, body kept facing well forward, *right knee gradually bending* (slightly only). (9) When hands are in to chest, turn body until facing square to stern, left foot touching bottom, and taking weight. (10) Arms shoot (or push) out towards stern, weight of body thrown backward on pole. (11) Recover body, arms and pole, and left foot until position 1 is assumed, hands keeping their position on the pole."

He adds:

"The hands should not drop below the level of the chest at the end of the shove unless, of course, the water is so deep as to necessitate this."

At full pressure, the shove is made with the hands close together on the pole, not moving till the shove is completed. Winstanley's is an excellent description of the old racing stroke, beginning with the pick up in three.

The illustrations on the next page are of the punting stroke at full pressure in a racing punt punted from the centre, but with a recovery or pick-up in three. The forward foot always remains stationary. The illustrations should be of help to a beginner confident in handling the pole easily; but before this, learn control of the pole in an upright and relaxing posture. The movements are of the classic punting stroke.

The illustrations were drawn from photographs especially taken for the purpose by R.C. Bending (T.P.C. Champion 1946–9). Bending developed a very full body turn for the racing stroke, and a pleasure punter may not turn so fully as shown in these diagrams.

1. At the end of the shove, the hands, high and together, move away from the body to finish. The fingers relax on the pole and stretch out. (W10)

2. When the stroke has finished, the forward hand draws the pole forward, sliding it through the rear hand till the forward arm is almost horizontal. The rear foot moves forward. (W1 & 11)

3. The rear hand grips the pole and throws it forward with a swing over the forward hand returning to catch it below at about the point of balance (W2 & 3)

4. The forward hand carries the pole forward, controlling its height; the rear hand controls its angles (fore-and-aft and lateral) pushing it forward and down to the position for the throw. (W4.i)

The punter is standing at the centre of a 2ft racing punt with a 12ft pole in about 3ft of water. The illustrations will be of help to a beginner who is confident in handling the pole easily. Before this, master control of the pole in an upright and relaxed position. Learn on dry land, if necessary.

5. *The forward hand throws the pole down, its position precisely placed by the rear hand. (W4.ii)*

6. *As the pole reaches the bottom, the rear hand grips the pole high. (W5)*

7. *With the pole firmly in the bottom, the forward hand grips the pole closely above the rear hand; the pull of the hands towards the centre of the chest begins. (W6 & 7)*

8. *The hands cross the centre of the chest. The body begins to turn. The rear foot moves back and begins to take weight. (W9)*

Always, *when punting standing still, the forward foot should be against the side of the punt, preferably against a knee, and should never move from that position.*
In position 1, the finish, there is an error in the drawing, the pole resting on the punter's shoulder; the pole should touch the outside of the shoulder.

Double Punting

Double punting was at one time a common practice in pleasure punting. It is of course still a usual event in punt racing. Pleasure punts would often carry a spare pole slung in leather straps over the side of the punt; this could be used for double punting. For a long trip, double punting can considerably reduce the physical effort needed for it. The rhythm developed from good timing can give the punters a great deal of pleasure and satisfaction.

For double punting, the punters may punt from opposite sides or from the same side. Punting from the same side is better; punting from opposite sides is less efficient, since the punt lies flat on the water and does not have the keel to give directional stability obtained by keeping the weight on one side; nor does it so well assist good timing. Bow gives the timing of the stroke and the stern man is mainly responsible for steering; otherwise for steering, bow pole shoves around and the stern pole pinches the punt.

A beginner may do well in learning to punt by double punting with a skilful and considerate punter. A beginner double punting should punt at bow; the stern man should be competent to keep in time whatever timing is given and should undertake the steering. (When the beginner starts learning to steer from stern position, it may help at first for bow to put in two strokes to stern's one, and correct the direction on the alternate stroke.) In double punt racing, perfect timing is required, particularly in moving the foot. To stop up, bow gives a signal to stop punting and turn. Stern then becomes bow, and must give a signal or call for throwing down the poles: the poles must strike the bottom simultaneously and at the same angle.

Punting Facing Forward

This technique is sometimes to be seen and is common at Cambridge when the punter stands on the stern. It is mechanically less efficient than standing square to the side; it would only be used by a professional Thames waterman when manoeuvering a punt in a limited space. There were no professional watermen who taught punting when it was introduced at Cambridge and undergraduates developed *ad hoc* a method most convenient for novices. A leading professional Cambridge waterman was in fact taught the Thames style of punting by an undergraduate from Maidenhead when punts were introduced there, and the Thames style appears to have been used almost only by undergraduates who had first learnt to punt on the Thames. When standing square to the front, the pole can be brought up in three, but the shove consists of a pull without the push or after-shove that follows in the full stroke; the stroke is mechanically lengthened a little sometimes by bending the knees and pulling the hands down to the feet, the recovery being made with a spring upwards which may rock the punt. The technique is not effective for racing because the stroke is too short, lacking a back-shove; nor does the pole travel for long enough along the side for steering-leverage. Steering must therefore be done by trailing the pole over the stern, losing both time and momentum from pole-drag.

One-Armed Punting

This was once a popular technique used in less serious regattas. The punter stands facing squarely forward and brings up the pole by throwing it forward two or three times to the point of balance where it can be tilted with a wrist movement. Reaching the vertical, the pole balances easily and can drop. Steering during the shove is not difficult.

At the end of the shove, direction can also be corrected with a small twist of the wrist when the pole has floated to the surface. Keep the feet still throughout, but bend the knees to create a rhythm.

Punting with Hands Low

This is a technique which was used for pleasure punting in the 1890's, and possibly developed earlier; for Leslie mentioned the importance of keeping the hands low in order to keep the wrists dry, in *Our River*. The technique contrasts with that of the conventional stroke for punting at pressure, for it has a simple, single purpose which decides the matter of style: to produce the maximum mechanical efficiency with the minimum of physical effort, effortlessness receiving first attention. In the days when men punted with starched cuffs, the technique was valuable for keeping the wrists dry. From a distance, a punter using the technique might appear almost motionless and certainly effortless. The technique is excellent practice for maintaining an upright posture.

The technique may be learnt by following this strict drill: both arms are stretched at full length downwards and the hands are bent up at right angles to the wrists. For practice, the whole stroke can be made with the hands well below the waist; the effort is worth attempting. A well shaped and balanced pole, tapered towards the top, helps. Hold the pole precisely horizontal and test its balance. Hold it with the rear hand over it; and with the forward hand over when the point of balance is to the rear of the rear hand, and under it when it is forward of the rear hand. Keep the point of balance near the rear hand. With the point of balance carefully controlled, the pole will swing easily to the vertical position with a downward pressure of the rear hand and an upward pressure of the forward, the arms still stretched well downwards. After the pole is dropped, the shove can be made with the arms low and the wrists bent up; when the pole has floated to the surface, the recovery is made hand to hand in their lowest position.

The stroke may be made at greater pressure after the drop, still keeping the wrists dry, by pulling on the pole with the rear hand first, and then as the body passes the pole, the forward hand following it at waist height; the rear hand following again, until the pole has passed to its full length. This is in fact "climbing the pole", though on a horizontal plane. The forward hand can grip the end of the pole as it floats to the surface with the wrist over the end of it, a grip similar to the forward hand on a cricket bat. With the hands low, the recovery may be made vigorously, accelerating on the second movement. Then if as the pole is accelerated, the forward hand, held open, is brought sharply back and slightly downwards as the pole accelerates, it lifts quickly and effortlessly to the position for the drop, with the forearms at waist height. When the technique is completely mastered, it is no more effort to punt sitting down than standing up. If the punter has gone on the river to be idle, this allows longer periods between strokes than would be needed with a paddle. The pole can be held with the hand resting on the side between strokes, its weight carried by the water. The recovery can be made with the forward hand resting on the side, the pole sliding over the fingers as they droop below the side. A brief acceleration will lift the pole as the slightly open forward hand is pulled back against it. Steering during the stroke is easy because of the forward position of the punter in the punt. The punter is out of any difficulties made by a cross-wind, and the occasional shove with a pole requires considerably less effort than the constant use of a paddle.

65

Rotating the Pole

The "windmill" stroke made by rotating the pole, with alternate ends striking the bottom, is occasionally seen. It should not be encouraged without a special pole for it, since this could damage the unshod end. In water about a foot deep, the windmill stroke would be in theory very efficient made with a special suitable short pole, but there is very little water suitable for it. The stroke has been tried on part of the present Chertsey course just above the old Shepperton course. American canoe-polers have experimented with the windmill stroke. A three-quarter rotation of the pole can be used for stopping-up, the shoe passing overhead. A former Thames Punting Champion used to make several windmill strokes at the end of a less serious race to indicate he had won. Abel Beesley is said once to have rotated the pole when he had a very unequal competitor and also stopped to talk to the spectators.

Grappling Punts

Several punts together can be moved by one punter if they are grappled by the passengers or tied together by painters. If grappled, the best place to hold is near the forward back-rests. A number of punts held together thus can be double punted from opposite sides. To travel a long distance it is easier to tie the punts together with their painters. This is called rafting them.

Punting a Dinghy

In the right circumstances, a waterman may handle most craft with a pole and should feel he will do so without difficulty. A dinghy is the craft he is most likely to handle thus. How it is handled will depend on its design; but many dinghies are more easily punted stern first. At one time in children's regattas, punting dinghies stern first was a popular event, and many young watermen learnt to punt this way.

In water suitable for it, a dinghy is more manoeuverable when handled with a pole than with oars or sculls. The waterman looks ahead and can also see easily all around him; the pole occupies only a few inches of space around the craft, whereas oars or sculls extend to double their length around it; with a pole, the waterman can make small and precise movements; though not suitable for speed or distance, paddling with the pole can replace shoving in an unexpected depth or mud patch. A seaman calls a pole used for this purpose a "sprit"; the word "spar" is more often used for timber in standing or permanent rigging.

Hints on Punting

H.M. Winstanley ended his book *Punting* with a few hints. They include: "Learn swimming before punting... Never go out in a punt without a spare pole or paddle. If your pole sticks hard in mud, let go! You can go back and fetch it... If you come to deep water, and have no paddle, you can paddle quite well with the pole... When you want to turn your punt round, let the stream help you. When you are going upstream, put the bow out into the stream and it will swing round of its own accord. Similarly, if you are going downstream, put the stern out into the stream... If you don't want to get wet, in lifting your pole out and dropping it into the water, use your fingers, not your whole hands."

Other writers on punting emphasize the importance of punting with the fingers. As far as possible, effort should be concentrated in them more than in the limbs and trunk. It is a good practice occasionally to punt with the fingers only in order to check the faults in style it can eliminate. With regard to keeping dry, A.E. Banham wrote, "if, in recovering and holding the pole, the backs of the wrists are kept up and the fingers and thumbs droop downwards, the punter should keep entirely free from the spray-bath effects when going at a moderate pace." He did not mean facing upwards, but high; the grip may be overhand or underhand, but the wrist position must be found to make the hands droop, as a pianist's hands should droop from the wrists. Handling the pole with the fingers only is another exercise suitable for practise on dry land, with the arms relaxed and the body upright.

A cross wind can affect steering and cause a good deal of difficulty, even for an experienced punter. The wind catches the area of surface of the body at the stern like a sail, turning it towards the lee bank, and the head of the punt into the wind. In a strong wind, the whole of the punt may move towards the lee bank as well. A beginner should therefore avoid learning in a cross wind. In difficulty, it may be well to use paddles.

Safety in Punting

Accidents in punting occur, and in recent years there have been deaths by drowning from punts. With good watermanship, moderate competence and a knowledge of conditions of danger and how to deal with them, punting is perfectly safe. Cambridge has a better safety record than Oxford; the fact that the river most used for punting at Cambridge passes through college gardens and the town and is better watched may help, but it is still liable to fast streams in flood water.

Deaths by drowning have been caused by drunkenness; those going on the river to drink must bear in mind that they may hazard a life; in one case, it was found that members of such a party could not afterwards tell the coroner how or when one of them who had drowned was missed; in such circumstances, therefore, danger is possible when little expected.

There are two conditions of danger from the stream. The first is a swollen stream, one found in spring or after prolonged heavy rainfall. If the punt gets out of control because of a fast flowing stream, it can be quickly, strongly and unexpectedly swung, and the punter who does not bring the pole to a position of safety is in danger. However, punt-hirers now usually prohibit the use of punts in a dangerous stream. The second danger is that for a punter surprised by falling in; if the water, again often in a swollen stream is murky he may lose his sense of direction, even if only briefly; danger is greater if he is carried under branches or vegetation.

Everyone punting should be able to swim; but surprise can add to danger and a punter should, from time to time, imagine what he would do if he or a passenger fell in. Anyone who falls in does so almost certainly because of a momentary over-exertion of some part of the body. The over-exertion preceding the fall can confuse and disconcert adding even more to the danger. If you have reason to believe you may fall, relax and make plans. It is better to fall in deliberately under control than later out of control. Fall feet first, take your bearings and decide in advance where you are going to swim to. The fact you do this may relax you enough to put you in a position of safety again. Experience of swimming fully dressed in a river is worth having. Some boat clubs have required members to swim in a mackintosh and boots. Another rule taught is, always to swim to the boat.

There are two conditions of danger concerned with the punter's style: first, punting with a foot away from the side, and secondly gripping the pole too hard. These are both natural faults for a beginner. They can become habitual and be incorporated into a style; for a style of punting once acquired and adhered to because it works, may be difficult to change.

With regard to the first danger, the novice should concentrate on keeping the centre of gravity of the pole outside or at least above the edge of the punt, not inside it. The further inside the punt it comes, the more dangerous it will be in a moment of danger. A novice sometimes tries to balance the punt so it is level crossways, believing it will help his balance; but it will not. A good exercise for establishing balance (one recommended to beginners by Winstanley), is to keep the toes of both feet against the side of the punt and to rock it gently until the feel of balance comes, from the toes, the ankles and legs, always being relaxed and "giving" at the knees. The knees and ankles should absorb all the movements of the punt like "shock absorbers" so that the upper body remains balanced and steady.

The second danger is probably the greatest of all, and the most serious — gripping the pole unnecessarily hard. This arises from the increase of body tension. It may be recognized or unrecognized. It may eventually cause so strong a grip on the pole that the punter can hardly move his arms, and so compulsive that the punter releases his hands with difficulty. It is very important to learn to relax the hands and fingers or reduce their tension at the end of every stroke as part of your style and technique. Tension, particularly in the hands, also causes the crouching, stooping or bending of the body or knees that is dangerous. It is often more apparent to an onlooker than to the punter. Anticipating danger in a punt, straighten your body and relax your arms immediately. This brings you at once to the position of greatest safety. Then bring the pole from wherever you are holding it to the lowest point at which you can hold it. Indeed, the reflex on touching a pole at any time when not making a stroke, should be to bring or slide the fingers to reach the lowest point at which it can be held. Let the pole float on the water, astern. In this position you can hold it with a finger tip only, if you wish; hold it with the least effort possible. Straighten your body. A safe position now is the "mid-recovery" position with the hands apart in front of the body and the pole at about 45°. When you are motionless and upright, begin to think what action is necessary. It may be a half shove. It may be to swing the punt with the pole. More important, however, is to maintain your posture and to eliminate unnecessary effort in action. Using more effort than you require is one of the principal causes of danger in punting and causes tension to increase. In a position of danger you will be safe with your hands at their lowest position.

There are two minor causes of danger in punting that should not provide difficulty: mud and tree-branches. If you have difficulty with mud, it is because you are using too much effort. Punt lightly with your fingers; develop a feel for the river bottom that comes through the use of the fingers. If there is no slight vibration as the pole strikes the bottom, beware that it may be soft. The best technique for punting in mud is to lean forward and put the pole into the water at 45° backwards. Push only gently. The combination of angle and a quick twist and tug will release the pole. If it goes in vertically, it will sink deeper into mud: therefore (1) low angle, (2) half-shove only, (3) light pressure, (4) twist and tug.

If the mud is hindering your progress, do not hesitate to use your pole like a canoe-paddle till you have passed it.

Looking well ahead, you can keep clear of most tree branches. If you have to punt under them, be sure to keep momentum in the movement of the punt and choose the right moment to give a shove towards them; then, holding the pole down at the second movement of the pick up, at the mid-recovery position, wait for a suitable place in the branches to lift the pole between them. When racing punts are crowded together, poles for safety should be brought to the vertical. This is a safe position also for the heavy pleasure punt pole, especially on land. Learn to hold the pole near its bottom, balanced vertically without support from the shoulder, hanging from your fingers with your arms stretched down.

The Rule of the Road

At sea or on inland waterways in every part of the world, the rule of the road is to keep to the right of oncoming craft. Most other rules are based on common sense; for example, a boat overtaking keeps clear of the boat it is overtaking, holds its course and speed and avoids crossing ahead.

At Oxford and Cambridge, by punting left-handed, that is to say, on the right as one faces forward, it is easier to follow the narrow streams of the Cherwell and Cam facing the bank, and the bank to the right is the correct one to follow. This may explain why it is customary on the Cherwell and Cam to punt left-handed. At one time the Thames Conservancy byelaws provided rules for punts. Their most recent navigation byelaws, those of 1957, omit them. In 1895 the rules said: *"Boats going against the stream.* – A rowing boat or punt going against the stream or tide has the right to either shore or bank, and should keep inside all craft meeting it (except barges towing). When going against stream or tide, and overtaking another craft, a rowing boat or punt should keep outside the craft overtaken." For boats going with the stream, the rule is the converse; but there is the following addition: "it would undoubtedly be a concession of considerable advantage to a punt to be allowed to pass on the inside close to the shore, more particularly in places where the river is deep in the middle … when going down stream punts should never claim to go on the inside as a right, but only take that position if the skiff is inclined to make way for them."

On rivers that are rowed on, punts can present difficulties to eight-oared, four-oared and uncoxed boats. Oarsmen prefer punts to keep to the banks, though boats will themselves sometimes come in to a bank. A good cox, in the interests of good watermanship, is keenly aware of all around him. If you have any doubt of a boat not seeing you or giving you room, shout early and very loudly, "Look out ahead!"

Give consideration to other punts, especially beginners who are trying to avoid you. If you are not certain of the course of an oncoming punt, hold your course to see how it will pass. Steer to pass it on the opposite side to your pole. The control of the situation will remain with the punt making the last shove; therefore delay your shove if in doubt. Give an oncoming punt as much room as it needs and always steer to avoid a collision if possible. If the other punt touches you, and you have delayed your shove, you will then have momentum to stay on course and very gently but precisely push the other punt aside, by steering against its weight, shoving around or pinching your punt to the degree to stay exactly on your course; do not push it further than you need for this. If you are compelled to make a shove within touching distance of another punt, it may be better to make a half-shove, not a full-shove, to keep the reserve of power it can give.

The History of Punts

Pleasure Punts Today

The pleasure punts of today were unknown before 1860. They reached their greatest popularity in Edward VII's reign (1901–1910). Between 1950 and 1970, they were driven off most rivers by the wash of increasing numbers of motor boats which rocked or swamped them. Today they are found almost only at Oxford and Cambridge on rivers protected for them. In 1939 there were 1,600 licensed motor boats on the Thames: in 1978, 13,000, an increase of eightfold. On other rivers the increase has also been substantial. The only pleasure punts remaining for hire without previous arrangements, except at Oxford and Cambridge, are six at Stratford-on-Avon (Rose), four, one a mahogany fishing punt, at Henley-on-Thames (Hooper), two Thames and four Medway 46 in-wide punts at Godalming, Surrey on the Wey, and a few small punts at Houghton Mill near St Ives on the Great Ouse. There are still a number of privately owned punts. At Durham University, four colleges each have a punt on one of the most beautiful stretches of river in England

The Thames Punt

The punt is a traditional Thames craft. Its design may be unique. There are many small, square-ended craft throughout the world, but their frames are usually box-shaped. The frame of the Thames punt, however, is like a ladder. Broad cross-pieces called "treads" join the two sides together across its bottom; this is structurally its frame. The treads at Oxford only are called "rounds", the name for the cross-braces between chair legs. A punt's bottom is made of soft wood and may be replaced several times during its lifetime. The sides of a pleasure punt are made of mahogany and the treads of teak. The treads and sides are joined by braces called "knees". A pleasure punt usually has eleven treads, is 24 ft – 26 ft long and 32 in – 34 in wide. A few punts were built with 13 treads and were 26 ft – 28 ft long. The ends are called "huffs". The bottom, with planks lengthways, is built first, shaped with slopes at each end called "swims", the treads and knees are fixed to it and then the sides. The knees are either upright or "raked" or

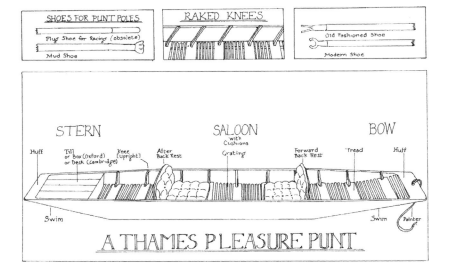

A THAMES PLEASURE PUNT

sloped; the sole purpose of raked knees is to improve the appearance. Between the treads, the floor is covered with "gratings". If a punt was narrow (as all pleasure punts are), the stern was covered with wood to strengthen the frame. This covering is called the "till" or sometimes (at Oxford only) the "box" and (at Cambridge) the "deck".

A racing punt, being even narrower, is covered at both ends; its coverings are called "counters".

The Thames Punting Club provides this useful definition of a punt in the rules of punt racing: "A punt is a flat-bottomed craft without stem, keel or sternpost, and the width at each end must be at least one-half of the width at the widest point. The length of a punt is its extreme measurement over all, and its width is its extreme part measured inside on the bottom. Subject to compliance with these definitions, a punt may be any length or width." The correct waterman's term for punting is "shoving", still used in punt racing.

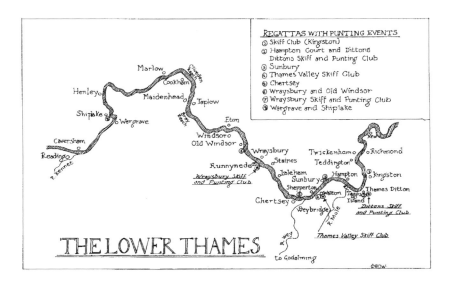

THE LOWER THAMES

Different Kinds of Punts

Until 1770, the Thames was much shallower than now. A great deal of its bottom is gravel. The punt was a useful craft then, easy to manoeuvre, capacious and able to move in very shallow water. After 1770, river improvements began. More and better locks were built to control its depth, and channels were dredged for navigation and to contain the water in floods. Punts of different kinds were used for different tasks. The largest were barges, sometimes with a sail, able to sail in the shallow parts of the Thames estuary and over the mud flats of the east coast, and called at sea "swimmies". Before the building of bridges, there were many ferry punts of different sizes. Ballast punts dredged gravel, valuable for road making and building, from the river bed. Watermen used punts for transporting goods between houses and villages along the river when it was more suitable for this than roads. Work punts were used for the repair of river banks and locks. Finally, there were many fishermen working on the river until fish stocks diminished. Net fishing was prohibited by the Thames Conservancy, founded in 1857. Fishermen used a special design of punt, the fishing punt.

The word "punt" was originally used for any small craft. A number of its uses were replaced during the 19th century by the word "dinghy", introduced from Bengal. By the early 20th century its use was largely restricted to the Thames craft. Some examples of its older use are "gun punt", an obsolete, canoe-shaped, clinker-built wildfowler's craft (surviving as a Norfolk club sailing boat) and "Falmouth quay punt", a Cornish design of fishing yawl. A "duck punt" is a small, stemmed, flat-bottomed, sculling boat.

Punt Poles

Poles are used to shove craft of various kinds on inland waters in many parts of the world. They are especially useful for handling heavy canoes on rapid rivers. The broadland "quant" and Dutch *stok* differ from punt poles in having cross pieces at the top to place under the armpit when shoving. The first punt poles were heavy larch spars, roughly cut. The first pleasure punt poles were spruce, shaped and varnished, like today's. Racing poles weighed about 4½ lbs and were West Virginia spruce, a wood not available since 1936. From 1946, aluminium poles weighing 3¼ – 3½ lbs have been used for racing. The Lower Thames being shallow, poles used there were 13 – 14ft. A rough guide to depth was that above Cookham the Thames was deeper, and below it shallower, dredged channels excepted. Both at Oxford and Cambridge poles are 16 ft and weigh 9–10½ lbs; they are all made by F. Collar of South Hinksey, Oxford. At Oxford some aluminium poles are used of the same weight and length. A leaky aluminium pole, being hollow, fills with water and becomes heavier. The end of the pole is fitted with a metal "shoe". The earliest shoes were forked. The usual shoe now is of a double horned shape, supposed to prevent the picking up of stones. A fluted half-disc shoe is called a mud shoe, though on mud how the pole is used is more important than the shape of the shoe. For use on hard gravel, some racing poles had a rounded end called a plug shoe.

Fishing Punts

Today's pleasure punts and racing punts both originate from the fishing punt. The fishing punt was 24–25 ft long and 42–46 in wide. It had a short till and forward of the till, about one-third of the way along the punt, was a "wet well". The wet well was a watertight box across the width of the punt, about a foot wide, the same height as the punt and covered with a lid. At either end of the box, holes in the side of the punt flooded it with water; in it was kept the fisherman's live bait and sometimes catches of fish or eels. The fishing punt was built of oak, often tarred on the bottom, and was traditionally painted green. It was not built for movement, was wide enough to hold three chairs and was moored all day for fishing to poles called "rye pecks". There are now only four traditional, oak fishing punts left on the Thames, at Sunbury. The last statutory ferry punt shoved with a pole is also at Sunbury, but it is rarely used now.

The First Pleasure Punts

In the second part of the 19th century the railways made the Thames valley much more accessible to residents of the rapidly growing city of London. It became a popular place for recreation and residence by those who could travel to and from London. Residents beside the river began to have fishing punts built of mahogany, varnished not painted, for their own recreation. These varnished, mahogany fishing punts were lighter than oak punts and served the dual purpose of fishing and travelling for pleasure; the second purpose was often the more popular because, being light, they were easy to move. If passengers were carried, a mattress was placed against the till and sometimes also against the wet well (kept dry in a pleasure punt when not fishing). It was not until the 1880's that the "saloon" punt was invented with the seating design used today for four passengers or "sitters" looking inwards, leaning against "back-rests" and with specially fitted cushions to sit on.

Walking and Pricking a Punt

The building of lighter punts meant that it was possible to punt them standing still. This is called "pricking" the punt. The heavy oak punt was "walked" or "run". The punter dropped in the pole at the bow of the punt and walked down it at least three paces, pushing or "shoving" with the pole. This was very often necessary for handling a heavy punt. When the first pleasure punts were pricked, it was usual to punt stern first, from the open end opposite the till. In 1898, P.W. Squire, secretary of the Thames Punting Club, comparing the old type of punt with the new saloon punt, wrote "When the lounge cushion is placed against the 'till' or covered-in end of the punt, as in the old-fashioned style, the craft is usually propelled stern first." At Oxford, men continued to punt stern first after the saloon design of punt was introduced, and it is now traditional at Oxford to do so. Lord Desborough noted that when Abel Beesley first won the professional championship in 1878 by pricking his punt, he punted stern first. There are certain advantages in it for a learner also.   The saloon punt was probably more popular at first on the Lower Thames. Pleasure punts were not introduced to Cambridge till after 1900 and always have been of the saloon design only; like Thames punts outside Oxford, they were punted bow first, but not always from behind the after back-rest. Punters at Cambridge often stood on the till or deck, a position of advantage for beginners. Punting stern first is sometimes called punting from the "Oxford end" and bow first, from the "Cambridge end".

Early Punt Racing and the Giants of the Sport

Both professional watermen and amateurs raced punts from early in the 19th century. Punt racing was very popular at Eton College until 1852 when it was prohibited because punts were believed to be used for school vices, smoking and drinking. The first professional championship of the Thames was held over a one-mile course at Maidenhead in 1877, the Maidenhead Mile. The same course was used for it until the championship finished in 1953. The greatest professional punter of all time was Abel Beesley, an Oxford Waterman. The greatest of amateur punters was W.H. Grenfell, later 1st Lord Desborough, the "Grand Old Man of almost every kind of sport". He was president of the Oxford University Athletic and Boat Clubs, broke his school's half-mile record, twice swam the pool below Niagara Falls, made the ascent of five Alpine peaks in eight days, captained the British épée fencing team at the age of 49 and was president of the M.C.C., the L.T.A. and of the 1908 Olympic Games. He and Abel Beesley, his coach, are given the credit of establishing punt racing as a recognized sport.

The greatest of women punters was Penny Chuter, ladies' amateur punting champion from 1957 to 1966, daughter of a retired naval officer at Laleham-on-Thames. She began skiff racing in 1958, best boat racing in 1959 and in 1960, aged 17, was placed 4th in the European Ladies' Sculling Championship as a member of the Laleham Skiff and Punting Club (since closed). She is now Senior National (A.R.A.) Men's Rowing Coach.

The Thames Punting Club

The Thames Punting Club was founded in 1887 at Sunbury-on-Thames. It took responsibility for the government of the sport of punt racing and organized an amateur punting championship. Grenfell reorganized the club in 1890 and in 1895 the club found an excellent punting course near Shepperton for its annual championship regattas. The course was inadvertently dredged in 1936 and lost; the regattas were held subsequently at Staines, Maidenhead and Laleham and were concluded in 1969 when competitors of sufficient standard were lacking. However, punt racing has continued by members of skiff and punting clubs affiliated to the Thames Punting Club in regattas held in August and September after the main rowing season has finished.

The Skiff and Punting Clubs

There are four clubs affiliated to the Thames Punting Club (the Thames Punting Club is also affiliated to the Amateur Rowing Association and the Skiff Racing Association). Punt racing is a very local sport, limited to the Thames from Wargrave below Reading to Teddington at the head of the London tideway, a distance of about thirty miles. There are about eight or nine annual regattas with punting events. The Dittons S.P.C. At Thames Ditton opposite Hampton Court; the Thames

Valley S.C. at Walton-on-Thames, and the Wraysbury S.P.C. at the east end of Runnymede are skiff and punting clubs. The Wargrave Boat Club is a social club with punt racing included in its activities. Anyone interested in seriously training for punt racing would be welcomed in a skiff and punting club, especially if competent in a pleasure punt and even more if experienced in punting a canoe. Annual subscriptions with use of boats are from £10 to £20. The clubs are open on Sundays, with two club evenings a week in the winter and four in the summer. There is an annual Inter-Club Punting Championship. It is hoped the amateur championship may be restarted.

Punt Racing

There are two types of racing punts: 2 ft wide punts for novice and doubles racing, and "best and best" punts for seniors and championships. The word best-and-best is an old boatbuilder's term for the best obtainable of the kind of boat required, not matched, as the 2ft punts are. A best and best punt is about 14 ½ in wide and 32–35 ft long. A punt racing course is 660–880 yards with a turn, so only half this distance of the river is used. The course should be shallow and firm, about 3–4 ft deep. The events are held in heats and the punts race in pairs. They are started from a stake-punt and turn at two poles called ryepecks, shod with iron points, planted in the river. Racing punts are double-ended, with both ends identical and are shoved from the centre. On passing the ryepeck, the punter "stops up", or stops the punt with his pole, reverses his direction (the bow becomes the stern) and passes up-stream on the other side of the ryepeck to finish where the race began at the ryepecks that were holding the stake-punt.

Dongola Racing

Exciting and popular events in punts are dongola races: the punts are paddled. The name commemorates Lord Wolseley's unsuccessful Nile Expedition of 1884–5 to relieve General Gordon at Khartum. Wolseley had 800 naval Whalers built, crewed by soldiers, with teams of Canadian voyageurs to help them at the many rapids and cataracts on the hazardous journey up to the head of the province of Dongola. He offered a prize of £100 to the first battalion to complete the 370 mile journey. *The Times* described it as "The longest boat race in history". The first dongola race was held at Maidenhead in 1886, with crews of eight, four aside with canoe paddles. A dongola crew today is usually six, mixed, four men and two women. The major trophy is the African World Shield, competed for at the Sunbury Regatta. At the Wargrave and Shiplake Regatta in 1981 there were entries from no less than 62 dongola crews. Dongola racing is traditionally light-hearted and crews often sink a punt at the end of the races, but serious dongola racing can produce displays of fine watermanship.

Long Distance Punting

In recent years, undergraduates from both Oxford and Cambridge have set up long distance punting records travelling mainly on canals, using camping punts, popular 70 years ago. Their reports are favourable and it may be that outside Oxford and Cambridge the most hopeful future for pleasure punts will be on canals. Most canals have a firm bottom for much of their width and at the few places where a bank is muddy there is always a hard bottom in the centre of the canal. There is an even depth at a convenient 6–8 feet. The reaches are straight. River traffic is slow, creating no problems with wash. As compared with some owners and hirers of river launches, the users of the canals are considerate, polite and usually show interest in traditional craft.

A camping punt is an ordinary pleasure punt with removable hoops 4 ft high; fitted canvas is unrolled over the hoops to turn the punt into a tent at night; the cushions fit the floor between the back-rests to make a mattress.

Printed in Great Britain
by Amazon